Sandra and her amazing daughter, Allie, have given us moms such a great resource to help strengthen our mother-daughter connection. *Meet Me in the Middle* captures real-life issues to help us navigate our relationship through those tricky teen years. This book will sharpen you both spiritually and relationally!

Amy Groeschel, cofounder, Life.Church; founder, Branch15, a nonprofit ministry providing care to women

Having two daughters of my own, I would've loved to have had this tool to help navigate the tween and teen years more effectively. My daughters are fabulous women, my dearest friends, and I still believe we could benefit from these lessons today! I don't just recommend Sandra and Allie's book; I think it is a must-read for mothers and daughters everywhere who desire a stronger connection.

Pamela Gregg Foxworthy, Bible study leader; wife to comedian Jeff Foxworthy; mother; grandmother; Jesus follower

Goodness gracious, I could have used this study when raising my two daughters through their teens! I'm fifty-eight and a grandmother, and my heart sometimes aches for my little thirteen-year-old self. She sure could have used this. What a sweet, thoughtful, and open discussion to guide you and your daughter through a really tricky, sometimes painful, but also beautiful chapter in your lives.

Leanne Morgan, American stand-up comedian; actress; author

Mamas and daughters, do not skip a single word of this book! As a mom to two girls—still in the thick of it with a rising ninth grader—I can tell you this for sure: no other book has brought both perspectives this well! *Meet Me in the Middle* is the guide every mom and daughter must read together. You will walk away armed with tools and practical advice to guide you during challenging times. I suggest you dog-ear Allie's endlessly useful "Rules for High School" now. Beyond that, this book will lead you both toward growth and victory in your relationship with each other, God, and your community as a whole.

Suzy Karadsheh, *New York Times* bestselling author; founder, TheMediterraneanDish.com

*Meet Me in the Middle* is a beautifully written book by both mother and daughter that helps bridge the gap to a long and rich relationship. All mothers desire a close relationship with their daughters, and daughters want their moms to understand and be proud of them. Sometimes as much as the desire is there, the connection is lost because neither knows how to make the connection. This book provides real-life practical tools to develop a long-lasting and fulfilling relationship between mother and daughter.

Karen Stubbs, founder, Birds on a Wire Moms

I'm a mother to four daughters, and this book is gold! Sandra and Allie offer biblical truth connected to the struggles and worries my girls have each faced in their middle and high school years in a way that opens conversations between mother and daughter that often feel hard to navigate. Allie's youthful, conversational tone speaks directly to the heart of both my older teens as well as my youngest, a soon-to-be tweenager. Her stories connect to their world and the pressures they often walk through. Sandra wisely takes us mothers by the hand and walks us through big doctrines like identity, forgiveness, and sanctification, giving us clear language for our own spiritual growth as well as that of our girls. The mom-and-daughter activities and discussions are so fun and easy to carry out that you will look forward to your time each week with your precious daughter! The investment of your time and energy will pay rich dividends in your relationship with your child.

Bethany Kimsey, author, *A Warrior Mama's Prayers*

Sandra and Allie have given mothers and daughters an incredible gift through *Meet Me in the Middle*. They've laid out a clear blueprint for navigating the teen years and intentionally nurturing the mother-daughter relationship. Implementing the truths found in this book will pay relational dividends years down the road!

Amy Rainer, teacher; founder, Etiquette with Amy

This book is filled with lots of Scripture and thoughtful cues to help you and your daughter love Jesus and each other better. Allie and Sandra show us that the same truths—*his* truths—that help us run businesses, navigate illnesses, or even deal with difficult people are even apparent in the most tender of relationships between mothers and daughters.

Mandy Cathy, Andrew's wife; mom to four kids who keep her on the go

# MEET ME
# IN THE
# MIDDLE

# MEET ME IN THE MIDDLE

## 8 Mother-Daughter Conversations about Life and Faith

Sandra Stanley & Allie Stanley Cooney

ZONDERVAN BOOKS

ZONDERVAN BOOKS

*Meet Me in the Middle*
Copyright © 2024 by Sandra Stanley and Allison Cooney

Published in Grand Rapids, Michigan, by Zondervan. Zondervan is a registered trademark of The Zondervan Corporation, L.L.C., a wholly owned subsidiary of HarperCollins Christian Publishing, Inc.

Requests for information should be addressed to customercare@harpercollins.com.

Zondervan titles may be purchased in bulk for educational, business, fundraising, or sales promotional use. For information, please email SpecialMarkets@Zondervan.com.

ISBN 978-0-310-36869-4 (audio)

Library of Congress Cataloging-in-Publication Data

Names: Stanley, Sandra, 1966– author. | Cooney, Allie Stanley, 1996– author.
Title: Meet me in the middle : 8 mother-daughter conversations about life and faith / Sandra Stanley and Allie Stanley Cooney.
Description: Grand Rapids, Michigan : Zondervan, 2024.
Identifiers: LCCN 2024008500 (print) | LCCN 2024008501 (ebook) | ISBN 9780310368670 (trade paperback) | ISBN 9780310368687 (ebook)
Subjects: LCSH: Mothers and daughters—Religious aspects—Christianity. | Mothers—Religious life. | Teenage girls—Religious life. | Christian life. | BISAC: RELIGION / Christian Living / Family & Relationships | RELIGION / Christian Living / Parenting
Classification: LCC BV4529.18 .S735 2024 (print) | LCC BV4529.18 (ebook) | DDC 248.8/45—dc23 /eng/20240404
LC record available at https://lccn.loc.gov/2024008500
LC ebook record available at https://lccn.loc.gov/2024008501

*Cover design and illustration: Emily Weigel / Shutterstock*
*Interior design: Denise Froehlich*

*Printed in the United States of America*

24 25 26 27 28 LBC 5 4 3 2 1

# Contents

## For Moms

*Introduction for Moms* . . . . . . . . . . . . . . . . . . 3
Chapter 1   Foundations Matter . . . . . . . . . . . 9
Chapter 2   You Are Who *God* Says You Are . . . . . . . . . .19
Chapter 3   No Win in Comparison . . . . . . . . . . . .31
Chapter 4   Family Is Forever . . . . . . . . . . . . . . .43
Chapter 5   Finding Your People . . . . . . . . . . . . . .57
Chapter 6   Fear Is *Not* in Charge . . . . . . . . . . . . . .71
Chapter 7   Peace in the Chaos . . . . . . . . . . . . . . .81
Chapter 8   Writing a Good Story . . . . . . . . . . . . 97
*Final Thoughts for Moms* . . . . . . . . . . . . . . . .109

## Meet Me in the Middle

*Introduction to Meet Me in the Middle Discussions* . . 115
Activity 1   Foundations Matter . . . . . . . . . . . . . 117
Activity 2   You Are Who *God* Says You Are . . . . . . . . . 121
Activity 3   No Win in Comparison . . . . . . . . . . . . 123
Activity 4   Family Is Forever . . . . . . . . . . . . . . . 125
Activity 5   Finding Your People . . . . . . . . . . . . . 127
Activity 6   Fear Is *Not* in Charge . . . . . . . . . . . . 131
Activity 7   Peace in the Chaos . . . . . . . . . . . . . . 133
Activity 8   Writing a Good Story . . . . . . . . . . . . 135

## For Daughters

|  | Introduction for Daughters | 141 |
| Chapter 1 | Foundations Matter | 147 |
| Chapter 2 | You Are Who *God* Says You Are | 157 |
| Chapter 3 | No Win in Comparison | 167 |
| Chapter 4 | Family Is Forever | 177 |
| Chapter 5 | Finding Your People | 189 |
| Chapter 6 | Fear Is *Not* in Charge | 201 |
| Chapter 7 | Peace in the Chaos | 211 |
| Chapter 8 | Writing a Good Story | 221 |
|  | Final Thoughts for Daughters | 229 |
|  | Acknowledgments | 233 |
|  | Notes | 235 |

# FOR
# MOMS

Rejoice in the Lord always. I will say it again: Rejoice!
Let your gentleness be evident to all. The Lord is near.
Do not be anxious about anything, but in every situation, by
prayer and petition, with thanksgiving, present your requests to
God. And the peace of God, which transcends all understanding,
will guard your hearts and your minds in Christ Jesus.

Finally, brothers and sisters, whatever is true, whatever is noble,
whatever is right, whatever is pure, whatever is lovely, whatever
is admirable—if anything is excellent or praiseworthy—
think about such things. Whatever you have learned
or received or heard from me, or seen in
me—put it into practice. And the God
of peace will be with you.

**—PHILIPPIANS 4:4–9**

# Introduction
# for Moms

Hi, mom!

Allie and I are so glad you're here. Let me tell you why.

Nervous is probably an understatement for what a lot of moms feel as they enter the early teen years with their daughters. As those moms gingerly peer through the curtains at the upcoming five or six years, they are all but shaking in their increasingly "chosen for comfort" shoes. They're nervous either because of memories from their own teenage years or because of their own interactions with their moms. Or they're nervous because of the stories they hear from the moms just ahead of them. Navigating all the internal struggles teen girls face is not for the faint of heart, especially in the current cultural climate.

We hope *Meet Me in the Middle* will be a tool for you and your middle school or early high school daughter, or young lady in your life, to use as you step toward each other and engage in conversations, activities, and outings that pave the way to connection.

You'll discuss:

- laying a faith foundation
- finding your identity and self-worth in Christ
- avoiding the comparison trap
- navigating family relationships
- navigating relationships with friends and boys
- facing fears
- dealing with stress and pressure
- making decisions

It is our hope that discussing these particular topics will impact this season of life and also set a precedent for future seasons of faithfully following the ways of Jesus.

You can do this study in eight consecutive weeks or spread it out in a way that works with the rhythm of your life and family. In preparation for each time together, you'll read the chapter written by me, and your daughter will read the one by Allie. Feel free to cheat and read hers too, if you're so inclined. I won't mention it.

In the center of the book, you'll find a section called "Meet Me in the Middle." After you've each read your chapter on a particular topic, you and your daughter will connect through the purposefully planned questions and activities related to that topic, found in the "Meet Me in the Middle" section. We want to help you break the ice, maybe get you laughing, direct your conversations, and point you both to Scripture.

We also hope that as your daughter moves through the transitions ahead, you can circle back and discuss some of these topics again. There's a big difference between what a fifth or sixth grader is experiencing and what that same young lady will navigate as a tenth or eleventh grader. Maybe be proactive and put a reminder on your calendar for two or three years from now. Pick the book up again with your daughter. I bet you'll both be entertained by looking back, as well as freshly challenged in some of the same areas.

The first two chapters are a bit more theological than the others because they lay a foundation of faith. The remaining chapters are more topical. I believe the solid foundation of the first two chapters will set you both up to see more clearly as you talk through just about any other tricky topic!

As you move through these chapters and have conversations and interactions with your girl, you'll see that Allie and I share Scriptures from all over the Bible. But one passage Allie and I were reminded of is especially meaningful in our own mother-daughter story—Philippians 4:4–9:

> **Rejoice** in the Lord always. I will say it again: Rejoice! Let your gentleness be evident to all. The Lord is near. Do not be anxious about anything, but in every situation, by prayer and petition, with thanksgiving, present your requests to God. And the peace of God, which transcends all understanding, will guard your hearts and your minds in Christ Jesus.
>
> Finally, brothers and sisters, whatever is true, whatever is noble, whatever is right, whatever is pure, whatever is lovely, whatever is admirable—if anything is excellent or praiseworthy—think about such things. Whatever you have learned or received or heard from me, or seen in me—put it into practice. And the God of peace will be with you.

We mothers desire for our daughters to move along—to progress—in their faith journey. In this book and the corresponding interactions, we'll be talking a lot about their hearts and minds. Rejoicing, having a gentle spirit, not being anxious, dwelling on things that are honorable, right, pure, lovely, commendable, excellent, praiseworthy—these topics all make frequent appearances throughout the book.

Why? Because what we dwell on and what we give attention to impacts our emotions and our actions. Our spiritual formation, and that of our daughters, hangs on what's happening in our own minds and hearts. And the way we think and what we believe play out in our actions—good or bad.

So much so that King Solomon, the wisest man ever to live (besides Jesus, of course), said in one of his proverbs, "Above all else, guard your heart, for everything you do flows from it" (Proverbs 4:23). The New American Standard Bible translates the same verse this way: "Watch over your heart with all diligence, for from it flow the springs of life."

Our hearts are the very source, or foundation, from which our actions, our words, our decisions, and our perspectives flow. We want our girls to excel in guarding theirs. We want them to consistently and diligently watch over their hearts. And we need to do the same with ours.

So how do we do that? How do we lead our girls there? Glad you asked! The foundation of faith, and of a Jesus-following journey, begins with salvation. Understanding who God is and what he did for us *through Christ* is where we start.

The God who created the world and everything in it, including you and your precious girl, loves big. But we have a sin problem that separates us from a relationship with him. In his great love, he made a way to repair the damage, to reconcile us to himself.

Take a look at these three verses of Scripture:

**God** demonstrates his own love for us in this: While we were still sinners, Christ died for us. **(ROMANS 5:8)**

**In** him we have redemption through his blood, the forgiveness of sins, in accordance with the riches of God's grace that he lavished on us. **(EPHESIANS 1:7–8)**

**Very** truly I tell you, the one who believes has eternal life.
**(JOHN 6:47)**

These verses are *everything*. Read them slowly—even try to memorize them—and let their truth find permanency in your heart.

Another verse, and the one Allie is using in the girls' intro, states all of this concisely and in a smaller package. John 3:16 sums it up simply: "For God so loved the world that he gave his one and only Son, that whoever believes in him shall not perish but have eternal life."

In his book *The Search for Significance*, Robert S. McGee talks about our justification through Christ: "Justification means that God not only has forgiven me of my sins but also has granted me the righteousness of Christ. Because of justification, I bear Christ's righteousness, and I am therefore fully pleasing to the Father (Romans 5:1)."[1] We are officially declared "not guilty" but instead are righteous before God because Christ paid the penalty for us—for all our past sins, our present sins, and, get this, our future ones too!

Your value to your heavenly Father is incomprehensible. If you've never done it before, find a quiet place or a quiet moment, bow before him, and accept his most precious gift—the redemption of your soul through the death and resurrection of Jesus. If you're not sure what to say, you can pray this simple prayer:

*Heavenly Father, a simple thank-you seems so small for a gift so enormous. I am filled with gratitude for the salvation you offered through the death and resurrection of your Son, Jesus. I humbly accept your gift. It's certainly a mystery that you no longer hold my sins against me. Thank you that in your eyes I am forgiven and clean. I belong to you.*

Through this most extraordinary act, God declares once and for all that you are worthy. You are valuable. You are precious to him. And so is your daughter.

In Allie's intro for your daughter, she'll explain and lay out this same salvation message. This just might be the most important conversation you ever have with that girl you love so much.

And by the way, you *both* have been prayed for!

So let's get started.

# CHAPTER 1

# Foundations Matter

I come from a long line of women who know how to cook. Both of my grandmothers could create amazing meals. I'm talking meat, three vegetables or side dishes, and a dessert. *Twice a day*. Oh, and they whipped up a pitcher of sweet tea somewhere in all that kitchen magic.

And then there's my mom. Ditto on the amazing meal skills for her but add in her homemade sourdough bread that was made fresh every week from a "starter" that lived in the fridge. It looked like a science experiment, and I was always a little scared of it. I would give it sidewise glances when I reached in for the milk and beg it not to come out and take over our home. It was "alive" after all. But Mom could make that stuff do amazing things. She had about a thousand variations of loaves, rolls, sticky buns . . . you name it.

Now fast-forward to newly married Sandra. Twenty-two years old and fresh out of college. Skill set: organization, the creation of efficient systems, a bit of accounting and finance, ease in making friends. Zero cooking skills.

However, what I lacked in skill, I made up for in confidence. Ignoring the fact that I had little to no meal planning or cooking experience, I decided that my husband, Andy, and I would host another couple at our house for dinner. I found a handful of recipes that looked easy. I went to the grocery store, bought some food, came home, and got to work.

It did not go well.

The meat was chewy and hard to swallow. The veggies were soggy and slimy. And why I thought a store-bought white cake with green gelatin and whipped topping was a good combo? I don't even know what to say about that.

The couple we invited over was polite and choked it down. And for whatever reason, they decided to remain friends with us. Nobody mentions that fateful meal, but I bet they haven't forgotten it.

I won't name names, but I was encouraged to enroll in a cooking course. So I signed up for Ursula's Cooking School in Atlanta and started my journey to understand food. By watching a professional, making notes, and then practicing the recipes at home, I started seeing smiles instead of trepidation when Andy, and others, took a seat at my table.

Why am I baring my soul and telling you this? Well, I had been *around* a lot of people who could cook. I set the table and sometimes put ice in the glasses, but I didn't participate in the cooking and preparation of any meals. I had no real experience with getting a meal on the table. It wasn't until I started learning and putting it all into practice that I could make food someone would want to eat!

While my story makes for an entertaining anecdote, this phenomenon is not limited to cooking. When it comes to our spiritual lives and how we live out our calling to follow Jesus, the same principle applies. Until we are intentional about understanding what it means to follow him and take steps to grow our faith, we might be *around* God, but we don't really know him or follow his calling for our lives. And we miss out.

And our girls miss out too. Because we can't impart to our daughters what we don't possess ourselves. We don't want our daughters just to be *around* God. We want them to have a relationship with God, through Jesus, that impacts not only their eternity but also how they live their lives. This relationship is the firm foundation that not only serves them well throughout their lives but also allows them to live lives that honor the God in whose image they were made!

So how do we get it right? How do we lead our daughters into a growing relationship with Jesus Christ? One that honors God, honors the people around them, and honors themselves and their futures? How do we move our girls toward having a foundation of faith that impacts their daily lives?

How do we help our precious daughter get to the place where:

- Her faith informs how she views herself and her worth.
- Her faith informs how she treats her family and friends and whom she chooses to date when that time comes.
- Her faith informs how she faces fears and the hard things that come her way.
- Her faith informs how she responds when comparison and stress knock at her door.
- Her faith informs her decision-making—both big decisions and small ones.

When our girls are faced with forks in the road and tough decisions, we want their faith to be the first responder!

So how do we get them there? What do we do?

The answer? It starts with us.

In the upcoming chapters of this book, we'll cover some topics and ideas that are practical and applicable for the next few years of your daughter's life. As you may well know, life delivers some bumpy circumstances and tricky situations. You have the honor of guiding and coaching her along the way. To do that successfully, and in ways that truly impact her, walking your talk is imperative. What you model for your daughter makes a larger impact than your words alone.

That said, I have some good news and some bad news. How about we start with the bad?

Bad news: Praying the salvation prayer from the book intro and coming to faith in Jesus Christ doesn't make all of life straighten out and our problems go away. There is no magic button to change our circumstances, and our lives don't instantly become problem-free. But you knew that already.

Now for the good news: We are *not* alone in our faith journey. A fancy theological word you might've heard before is *sanctification*. It simply means the process of becoming more and more like Jesus as we mature in our faith. And that is this book's primary purpose: to help you and the teen girl in your life move in the direction of the heavenly Father who loves you, the Savior who gave his life for you, and the Helper who is in it with you.

As I mentioned, we're not on the sanctification journey alone. And that's not just good news. That is *really* good news. Once we place our faith in the death and resurrection of Jesus, we have help. Actually, it's even better than that.

**We** have a Helper. God is present *with us* through the Holy Spirit.

When Jesus was preparing his disciples with the news that he was about to leave them, he knew they'd be distressed. He was their rabbi, their leader, the one they looked to for guidance and direction and instructions for what to do and when. And he was going away. But God. God always has a plan. Jesus comforted his followers by letting them know they were not being abandoned. In fact, an extremely competent Helper was on the way. This Helper has a lot of roles in the life of a Christian, a Christ follower. One of those roles is enabling us to "grow up" in Christ, to move along in our journey of sanctification. And as we do, we become more like Jesus every day.

John 16:13 tells us the Holy Spirit guides us into all truth. He helps us know what's true and what's not. And he also makes known to us what God wants us to know: "When he, the Spirit of truth, comes, he will guide you into all the truth. He will not speak on his own; he will speak only what he hears, and he will tell you what is yet to come."

In John 14:26, Jesus says the Helper will teach us and help us remember things he's taught us. He'll bring to our minds what we need, when we need it: "The Helper, the Holy Spirit, whom the Father will send in My name, He will teach you all things, and remind you of all that I said to you" (NASB). I could definitely use help with that!

In Galatians 5:22–23, the apostle Paul tells us that the "fruit" of the Spirit is love, joy, peace, patience, kindness, goodness, faithfulness, gentleness, and self-control. That means the Holy Spirit produces those fruits inside us. And we have them at our disposal to relate to the world around us. How amazing is that?

Something I know about myself is that I'm not super patient. I don't like to wait. I like efficiency and for situations to operate according to my plan and my schedule. When they don't, I get frustrated and begin to lose some of the fruits in that list.

I think I can safely say that most of my parenting fails were related to not being patient. Shall I make you feel a bit better about your own poor parenting moments? Okay, here's one: Allie and Garrett were around six and eight years old, respectively. They were outside playing, doing some fort building, probably. They loved forts. I was inside accomplishing *all the things* that were of utmost importance. Knocking out the to-do list. Slaying the household dragons. Possibly taking a little nap. I don't remember exactly. Anyway, in they came after a little bit of time, but not enough time because I wasn't done with my list or, ahem, nap. So I was a bit irritated. Garrett was hobbling along, supported by Allie. Apparently, he had climbed the brick gate column and jumped down onto the concrete driveway, barefoot.

I took a look. No broken skin. Maybe the beginning of a bruise. But I had stuff to do, so I assured him that he was fine and he'd probably have a heel bruise for a few days. Dr. Sandra diagnosis: heel bruise. "Here's some ice," I said. "Don't do that again." Fast-forward a week later. He was still limping. I was still busy. But I conceded, and we went to get an X-ray. Broken foot.

Aaaaannd Mom of the Year Award goes to? *Not* Sandra Stanley.

In the rearview mirror, maybe it's a little bit funny. But sometimes our impatience, or lack of other fruits, isn't funny at all. In those moments when the patience I can muster on my own is waning, or I'm standing in front of temptation and have a potential self-control problem, the apostle Paul says I can lean into what the Holy Spirit offers me and find exactly what I need, exactly when I need it. What a relief.

This is how we grow in our spiritual maturity. As we depend on the power and enablement of the Holy Spirit, our Helper, we are able to "grow up" in Christ. We become more like him. He lives in us and through us and impacts *every* part of our lives.

We say all the time at our church: "Following Jesus will make your life better and make you better at life." It's true. The more like Christ we are, the better our lives are. Not problem-free, of course, because we live in a world that delivers problems fairly frequently. But in the midst of it all, our lives are much better and richer and full of joy.

So how do we *do* that? How do we actually follow Jesus, and what does that even mean? He's not physically here for us to follow around, right? The process is pretty straightforward. It's an awful lot like the cooking illustration at the beginning of this chapter. First, we learn. We take in the information. We spend time reading the Bible, praying, listening to sermons, and using resources that teach us the truths of God's Word. Maybe we join a Bible study or a small group. As we do these things, the Holy Spirit meets us and does the work of planting God's truth inside us.

Our time alone with God—our personal devotional time, or quiet time—is a time when we pray. We make our requests known to God. Just like you love the connection that happens when your daughter shares her desires and hopes and wants with you, your heavenly Father also loves that connection with you.

This quiet time serves as the posture and the place where we do some of the things mentioned in the Philippians passage. We can rejoice, even when our circumstances aren't what we wish: job uncertainty, rocky relationships, illnesses. Paul reminds us that rejoicing is a choice and it paves the way to seeing our circumstances through God's eyes. And it happens when we spend time with God. "Rejoice in the Lord always. I will say it again: Rejoice! . . . Do not be anxious about anything, but in every situation, by prayer and petition, with thanksgiving, present your requests to God" (Philippians 4:4, 6). Time spent reading the Bible and praying is where we can lay aside our anxious thoughts and allow God to breathe calmness into our souls.

"Whatever is true, whatever is honorable, whatever is right, whatever is pure, whatever is lovely, whatever is commendable, if there is any excellence and if anything worthy of praise, think about these things" (Philippians 4:8 NASB). Pulling away to be with God, to read his words to us, is the best way to renew our minds and dwell on things that are true, honorable, right, pure, lovely, good, and praiseworthy. Then what we learn *about* God takes root in our hearts. And we *apply* what we've learned. Our faith begins informing how we live our actual lives. And this is where some amazing things happen. We begin seeing changes in our perspectives, our attitudes, and our behaviors.

When we're trying to live God's way, we obey what God says, even when it's hard. We start experiencing the benefits of obeying him and following his ways. We strengthen our faith muscle, and what's important to God becomes increasingly important to us. It's a transformation. Sometimes it's slow, sometimes not. Sometimes it feels like two steps forward and ten steps back. And sometimes the momentum is all forward. But we *are* growing and we *are* changing and we *are* maturing in our faith. And over time, following the way of Jesus becomes our default. There is no magic button to change our circumstances so that our lives become problem-free. But we find that we're not doing life alone. Our powerful God is *with us*, through the presence of his Spirit. And as the truths of God's Word take root in us, our lives begin to change.

I love what Nancy DeMoss says about her time alone with God in her book *A Place of Quiet Rest*: "When I get into His presence, the whole world looks different. When I draw close to His heart, I find mercy when I know I deserve judgment; I find forgiveness for all my petty, selfish ways; I find grace for all my inadequacies; I find peace for my troubled heart; I find perspective for my distorted views. In Him, I find an eye in the midst of the storm. Oh, the storm around me may not immediately subside, but the storm within me is made calm."[2]

Here's permission to think of yourself for a second . . .

Where are you in *your* faith journey? Where are you, really? Take a minute to ask yourself the following questions:

- Do I have a rhythm of time alone with my heavenly Father? A set time to be quiet and allow God, through the Holy Spirit, to make me more like Jesus?

- What changes do I need to make for that to happen more regularly? Going to bed earlier so I can get up earlier? Putting it on the calendar so I take it more seriously? "Coffee with Jesus. 6:30 a.m. Repeat every day, Monday through Friday." I'm kidding. Sort of. Actually, there was a season of my life when I did that.
- Can I designate a specific spot in my home for meeting with God, a spot where I can read my Bible and pray?
- Do I have a Bible of my own that is easy to read and study? What other tools do I need to have handy (a notebook or journal, pens and pencils, a commentary, etc.)?
- Do I have a mentor or friend who can encourage me and maybe even hold me accountable for prioritizing my devotional life?

A quiet time, or devotional time, or whatever you want to call it, isn't something to turn into a chore. Nor is it the key to obtaining God's approval. Your value and worth were established when he created you in his very image. And his approval of you was established when you were reconciled to God through the death and resurrection of Christ. That's all settled! You don't have to earn his love by checking boxes any more than your daughter has to earn your love that way.

When it comes to your time alone with God, he doesn't love you *because* you spend time with him. He wants to spend time with you *because* he loves you. He wants a real relationship with you, and he wants to show you how to export his brand of love to the people around you. He wants you to grow in your faith and in your practice of it. That's exactly what your quiet times, or devotional times, are meant to accomplish: meeting with your heavenly Father regularly and, during that time, allowing the Holy Spirit to move you in your growth journey to become more and more like Jesus Christ.

So where do you hope to lead your daughter? Do you want to help her lay a foundation of faith? Again, we can't impart to our daughters what we don't possess ourselves. So evaluate, make some adjustments if needed, and develop the kind of rhythm with God that you want your daughter to have. The rewards of growth and intimacy with God will be rich for you *and* for her as you become more and more like Jesus.

# CHAPTER 2

# You Are Who *God* Says You Are

I have a confession to make. I don't like dark chocolate. I want to like dark chocolate. I've pretended to like it. Cool people like dark chocolate. Disciplined people like dark chocolate. And I really want to be cool and disciplined. I love healthy living and healthy foods, and when you bundle those two together, that defines my hobby. Cooking healthy meals, working out, and even cleaning with products that have natural ingredients—I love it all. I just don't like dark chocolate.

Milk chocolate? Now that's a whole different story. I *love* milk chocolate. I've planned vacations around chocolate factories known for their legendary milk chocolate. It's smooth and creamy, and when you throw in some almonds or pecans or hazelnuts . . . goodness gracious! That is some decadent yumminess.

But to a lot of people who know me, this revelation will come as a shock. Because I've tried so hard. And I've pretended. To my eldest son, Andrew, who gave me dark chocolate for every occasion until he married a girl who upped his gift-giving game, I'd like to say, "I'm sorry I didn't tell you before."

There. I feel much better now that I've come clean and confessed.

Maybe you've pretended to like something or be something so that you could maintain a certain identity too. Maybe you pretended to like a certain kind of music, or particular types of books, or even distinct styles of clothing or hair. Maybe you took up a hobby to impress a person or a group, and you hated it but didn't quit because you wanted their approval and acceptance. Maybe you blew your budget and found yourself in financial hot water in a vain attempt to own something that would give you status and worth in the eyes of others.

Isn't it exhausting? Pretending to be something or someone we're not wears us out. Why do we do it? We do it because we're craving something. We're craving acceptance. Or we're craving approval. Or we're craving admiration. And we don't think we can get those without pretending or morphing ourselves into something we think might be a better version.

At the core of it all? We don't believe we're enough.

As Allie says in her message to your daughter, when we don't feel like we're enough, we usually turn to one of three options: We change. We pretend. Or we lose heart.

## We Change

When we change, we make the decision to switch into some other version of ourselves. We work hard to be different. We fight our wiring and the way God has uniquely equipped and prepared us. We strive. We join clubs or buy clothes. We borrow money for a better car or a bigger house. We try to change who we are to be enough in the eyes of others. The result is that we move so far from who we really are, and from the way God uniquely designed us, that we miss out on the things that will bring us true joy. The bigger risk is that we may miss God's best intentions for us—genuine lifelong friendships, a fulfilling career path, the kind of family we've always hoped to have, and opportunities to serve and love others in ways unique to us.

It's tough to watch our girls struggle and strive as they calculate pathways to acceptance that require them to be someone they're not. In their efforts to appease another person or group of people, they wear themselves out. As adult women who've been there, we know it doesn't work. At least not for long.

## We Pretend

Pretending is an awful lot like changing but with a bit more dishonesty involved. Maybe we believe we can't ever be enough, but we surely don't want other people knowing that. So we cover up. We cover up stuff about our past, even with safe people. We work hard never to let our new friends cross paths with our old ones. Certain topics of conversation are off the table with our families and our friends. Our bucket of secrets gets heavier and heavier, and it's hard to manage who knows what. We build a social media persona that isn't even close to who we really are because, in our minds, who we really are simply isn't enough.

The result of pretending is that our relationships suffer. One of the most important values Andy and I worked to instill in our kids was honesty. We told them all the time, "Dishonesty and lying *break* relationships." But as Allie tells your daughter, "It's even deeper than that. If you are not fully known, you won't be fully loved." If people love the pretend you, they aren't loving the real you.

## We Lose Heart

Allowing our worth to be evaluated and determined by anyone but God inevitably leads to a sense of hopelessness. When we buy the lie that we're not enough, and that we'll probably never be enough, we lose heart. We become discouraged and often give up. Feelings of insecurity and embarrassment are constant companions. We wallow in the awareness of our shortcomings, and soon finding a way out becomes harder and harder.

Quick on the heels of hopelessness is severely diminished self-worth and increased depression and anxiety. It doesn't take long for us or our girls to end up in dangerous places. The result of losing heart is that the door is slammed shut on the abundant life God has planned for us. It's a heartbreaking loss because his plans, like him, are so good. The life he offers is fruitful, fulfilling, and loaded with peace, even when things aren't perfect. But losing heart makes us miss out.

I wish it weren't innate in us to look around for approval, wondering how friends and acquaintances would sum us up if asked. The truth is, nobody actually asks them.

I wish it were not our default to work so hard at gaining acceptance from others, who themselves are also working so hard to gain acceptance.

I wish it weren't so natural to believe we need to perform a certain way or behave a certain way or look a certain way to earn admiration and affection from other people who are also busy performing, behaving, and working on their look.

It is so common, and startlingly easy, to fall prey to this. And I can't think of *anything* better to help your daughter avoid it than to have a clear understanding of how her heavenly Father—the one who created her in his image and breathed life into her lungs—views her and values her and loves her. If that idea becomes woven into the fabric of her life, and yours, it changes everything. I say let's do some weaving!

Our true value is based not on our behavior or the approval of others but on *what God says is true of us.* And here we encounter a big truth about him. It's made clear to us in the very first chapter of the very first book of the Bible.

*He made us.* God made us in his own image, in his likeness (Genesis 1:26–27). And he gave humankind purpose. That purpose was to image God to all of creation, to be the rulers of the other things God created: earth, plants, animals (Genesis 1:26, 28). God created humanity to have purpose and fulfillment and hope as they experienced fellowship with him and reflected him to the world around them.

But *we sinned* and broke the relationship. Purpose and fulfillment broke too. And along with all that, we got confused about our image. We mistakenly began looking elsewhere for purpose and value and worth. We started changing in our effort to find significance, and pretending in order to be worthy, and losing heart when it all fell apart. Our girls get confused about their image too. Their eyes rove, looking for approval from friends. Nothing feels more important than popularity. Being included, and not excluded, is the bull's-eye on the target—regardless of the cost. They change, pretend, and lose heart too.

Then *we were restored* to his image through Christ's death, resurrection, and payment for our sin. "Because of his great love for us, God, who is rich in mercy, made us alive with Christ even when we were dead in our transgressions—it is by grace you have been saved" (Ephesians 2:4–5). We didn't deserve this grace, nor did we earn it. He just chose to give it. He gave it by redeeming us from our sin and our brokenness through the death and resurrection of his only Son, Jesus.

Think about this. When God looks at you, he doesn't see a cleaned-up version of sinful you, or even a forgiven version of the you who is trying to do better. He sees you as his redeemed daughter. A *brand-new creation* with no scars, no spots, and no blemishes left over from your past. Your value to him is off the charts, and you don't have to perform. You don't have to earn *anything*.

And now *he gives us purpose.* That's right, he has given us back our purpose and paved the way to fulfillment and hope! Through the power of the Holy Spirit in us, we are to be God's image bearers every day, reflecting his character (love), his fruit (love, joy, peace, patience, kindness, goodness, gentleness, faithfulness, and self-control), and his ways to the world around us.

We don't just arrive at that destination though, right? When it comes to praxis—or the way our faith plays out in our everyday lives—there are two concerns: thinking and doing.

**Thinking:** We identify the lies others have handed us, or the ones we've placed on ourselves, and we replace those lies with the truth. Truth is what *God* says about us. Not what others say, or even what we default to thinking, but what *God* says.

**Doing:** Once we've straightened out what we think, we have a few questions to ask ourselves. How do we put what's true into practice and make it an active and real part of our everyday lives? What do we actually *do*?

Here are a couple of practical suggestions.

## Keep Truth in Front of You

Renewing our minds is an ongoing process. The cultural climate in which we live, the patterns and habits we've established over time, and the careless words of others (by accident or on purpose) all conspire daily to derail us from remembering who we are in Christ. *You* are his precious daughter. *Your girl* is his precious daughter too.

Having a quiet time is a super-important defense against believing those lies. So is memorizing pivotal Scripture verses or having them in our line of sight throughout the day—as wallpapers on our devices, under a magnet on the fridge, on note cards on our dashboard, or on sticky notes attached to our bathroom mirror.

The bathroom-mirror thing is Allie's favorite. Even though she doesn't live at my house anymore, I've kept a few sticky notes on the mirror in her old bathroom. The sticky residue reminds me of her commitment to memorize Scripture in high school. As tidy as I'm inclined to be, I can't bring myself to erase *all* reminders of that!

Spend a little time thinking about the best way to keep truth in front of you. Consider the routines and rhythms of your normal day. And spend a little time thinking about your daughter—her routines and rhythms too. How can you encourage her and coach her in the practice of keeping truth in her line of sight?

## Live Out Your Identity

In the following chapters of *Meet Me in the Middle*, we'll talk about all kinds of ways we can live out our identity and reflect God's image to the world around us. It's one thing to know our value and our worth and another to live it out. For now, let's take a look at our Philippians passage. It's full of practical ways to remember who God says we are:

> **Rejoice** in the Lord always. I will say it again: Rejoice! Let your gentleness be evident to all. The Lord is near. Do not be anxious about anything, but in every situation,

by prayer and petition, with thanksgiving, present your requests to God. And the peace of God, which transcends all understanding, will guard your hearts and your minds in Christ Jesus.

Finally, brothers and sisters, whatever is true, whatever is noble, whatever is right, whatever is pure, whatever is lovely, whatever is admirable—if anything is excellent or praiseworthy—think about such things. Whatever you have learned or received or heard from me, or seen in me—put it into practice. And the God of peace will be with you. **(PHILIPPIANS 4:4–9)**

In this passage, Paul paints a picture of what it looks like to live out your identity.

Several "to-do" gems are buried in these verses:

- **Rejoice.** Even when our circumstances seem bleak, there is power in rejoicing. We don't have to pretend to *like* the circumstances, but we can rejoice in the **truth** that God is with us in them. This is a way we can live out our true identity.
- **Be gentle.** When difficult situations catch us off guard, our knee-jerk response isn't usually gentleness. At least mine isn't. But if we pause and remind ourselves of the **truth** that God is with us, and in us, we can take a deep breath and respond with gentleness. This is a way we can live out our true identity.
- **Don't be anxious.** Wait, what? Can you even say that? Oh, okay, I'll just *not* be anxious . . . no problem. Seems impossible, right? We'll talk more about anxiety in a later chapter, but Paul is presenting the **truth** that an all-powerful God really does hold us near, even in anxious times. Reminding ourselves of that is a way we can live out our true identity.

- **Pray.** Many verses throughout the Bible point to the **truth** that God hears us when we pray. No prayer is unheard or not responded to by God. He will never ignore us. A posture of prayer is an invitation for our heavenly Father to meet us, to meet *with* us, and to whisper his affirmation and purpose into our souls. This is a way we can live out our true identity.

- **Dwell on the good stuff.** Paul just outlined what a bunch of the good things are. He lists them so we can take them in and begin to dwell on them and allow the **truth** of their goodness to transform us. He tells us to dwell on them because he knows our minds are where lies so easily take root. As we dwell more and more on the good replacements, those lies are dug up and thrown out. This is a way we can live out our true identity.

- **Emulate Paul, as he emulates Jesus.** Paul's story is amazing. He endured so much as he traveled around the Mediterranean rim spreading the gospel and helping churches get started. He was imprisoned, flogged, beaten, stoned, shipwrecked, endangered by rivers and bandits, sleep deprived, hungry, thirsty, and exposed to the cold (2 Corinthians 11:23–28). He wasn't bragging about all of that but simply pointing out that in the midst of it all, he persevered. He kept his eyes on Jesus and modeled himself after his Savior. Hopefully you won't experience any of those extremes, but life does deliver hard times to us. Paul demonstrated the **truth** of how Christians should live, even in harsh circumstances. He's a great example to follow. And as we follow, we live out our true identity.

Those are some pretty good ideas to get us going, right? So what does all this mean for you and your daughter exactly?

**To the changer:** You are enough. You don't have to work so hard at all the things, trying to morph into a different version of yourself. You can stop, take a deep breath, and know that you are made beautifully and purposefully in the image of the God of the universe. He declared your extraordinary value the moment he redeemed you. No more striving. No more searching. No more spending time and effort in vain to get to where God has already placed you. Welcome to the path that brings real friends, real purpose, and real fulfillment and joy.

**To the pretender:** You are enough. You don't have to hide anymore. You don't have to keep secrets. You no longer need to wear yourself out crafting posts and creating appearances. You can be honest now because your Father has declared your worth. You can be fully known and fully loved.

**To the hopeless:** You are enough. There is great hope for you. You can turn your eyes away from your fears and insecurities and gaze at the cross where Christ announced with his actions how "worth it" you are. And you can look forward to the abundant life God has promised you, the life that is full of fruitfulness, fulfillment, and peace—a peace so amazing it doesn't even make sense. "The peace of God, which transcends all understanding, will guard your hearts and your minds in Christ Jesus" (Philippians 4:7).

One last "mom thought" worth mentioning: Understanding that you are made in God's image and are called to reflect him to others involves knowing and understanding that God is loving and kind. But the ease with which we believe and can wrap our minds around the idea that God is loving and kind and wants the best for us is often proportionate to how loving and kind *our* parents have been to us. Whether we realize it or not, what parents model largely determines how a child views God. Good or bad. And that has huge implications for your relationship with your daughter.

Is there stuff in your own life that affects how you relate to your daughter and the tone you take with her? Are you carrying around any deep-seated issues that need dealing with more seriously? Anger issues? Lying issues? Do you lack some of the fruits of the Spirit—love, joy, peace, patience, kindness, goodness, gentleness, faithfulness, and self-control? Is their absence impacting your kids?

Think about finding a pathway to get help rooting out that stuff so you can better image your heavenly Father to your daughter. The Father, who is full of grace and mercy and kindness, and who has been exceedingly patient with you, wants your daughter to image him too.

You've got this, mama!

CHAPTER 3

# No Win in Comparison

I'll never forget the first time I found myself locked in the trap of comparison. Sometime around the third or fourth grade, as I was playing happily at recess with my friends, a boy called me "Bird Legs." I looked around for a bird but didn't see one. Then I realized he was talking about me! It was like a knockout punch to a skinny little girl. In that life-altering moment, I became aware of a feeling of being "less than." I immediately swallowed the bait and began to compare. I compared my legs with everyone else's for the next chunk of years. I didn't want to wear shorts or skirts. I was constantly comparing.

I was trapped.

And like the rest of humanity, I started taking my cues from the people around me. Guess what? I didn't outgrow that habit.

I bet you can rustle up a memory or two that catapulted you into the comparison trap as well. The things we compare change over the years, but the *tendency* to look around and compare doesn't. Every single day, we're tempted to glance to the left and glance to the right to see how we're doing, how we're measuring up to the folks around us.

And the trap doesn't stop with appearance. There is financial comparison, spouse comparison, vacation comparison, and even comparison of our kids to other kids around them—on the ball field, on the stage, in the classroom. For those of us who regularly check social media, the chronic struggle with comparing goes to the next level. And we're mature adults. Mostly.

Regardless of our age or stage of life, opportunities for comparison are always lurking. And it's easy to fall prey to the temptation. Whether those situations catch us off guard or are of our own making, the temptation to give in to comparison is real. When we do, it always leads to one of two outcomes.

First outcome: when we come up short in the comparison game, we feel "less than." We decide we don't measure up. We feel insecure, left out, or left behind. In some cases, we may feel God has shortchanged us. As much as we don't like to admit it, sometimes we even feel like he kept back something that he owes us. Jealousy and covetousness are quick to follow these feelings of insecurity. In your daughter's chapter, Allie uses the word *envious*. Envy sneaks in and wreaks havoc on the sincerity and health of our relationships. Here's what the writer of Proverbs says about envy: "A heart at peace gives life to the body, but envy rots the bones" (Proverbs 14:30).

Succumbing to envy after comparing and falling short wreaks havoc in our daily lives. It has real implications and consequences. Some of us are carrying debt because we stared at somebody else's lifestyle for too long. Some of us can't get along with our siblings because they have what we don't have. Some of us are physically sick because we've dieted ourselves to unhealth or worked ourselves beyond what's reasonable. Some of us are doing permanent damage to our relationships with our kids because we're driving them so hard to measure up to some unrealistic standard we've created, and we've dressed it up as "wanting what's best for them." And some of our marriages are suffering for the same reasons, just different details.

**Comparison** hurts us and hurts the people we care most about!

Second outcome: we find ourselves coming out on top. We feel "better than." Superior. We potentially become prideful or even judgmental. And just like with the falling-short scenario, our relationships take a hit. And we shouldn't think for a second that our precious daughters aren't picking up on this. They're probably following in our footsteps and quietly feeling superior to, or better than, some of the people around them. This won't serve them well—now or later.

Interestingly, in both of these comparison outcomes, we tend to forget all about our *actual* worth and value—the intrinsic worth that comes with being made in the image of a God who loves us and sent his Son to die for us.

Whether we're falling short or coming out ahead, most of us have become skilled at hiding the less attractive thoughts and feelings we have. Even from ourselves. We don't like seeing the ugly things inside us, right?

Speaking of ugly things inside us, have you ever secretly celebrated someone else's failure? I mean, you don't want to see them implode or have something terrible happen. But maybe your coworker could get skipped over for the promotion this time. Or maybe your friend could gain a little weight and finally understand what it's like to struggle. Even worse, have you hoped a friend of your daughter's might experience a failure so that you and your daughter can feel better about her situation? I know. It's ugly. But it's a real temptation at times. Feelings of jealousy and covetousness sneak into our hearts and minds and do their poisonous damage.

So what do we do? How can we keep our hearts clean and clear of the jealousy that comparison delivers? Hold tight and we'll talk about that in a minute.

What about our girls? Here's something you already know: your daughter struggles with comparison on some level. The severity may ebb and flow, but it's a real and daily battle. Somewhere along the way, she picked up on the universal habit of comparing herself to the people around her. And if she spends time on social media, she's bombarded daily with opportunities to compare. Filtering through what's real and what's not is tricky because everyone else appears to have it all together. Every day is a #bestday. And every challenge is met with victory. Otherwise, why post?

So our girls get chronic doses of feeling "less than" and often find themselves facing anxiety and even some level of depression as they try to measure up but fall short.

The good news? We know what it's like to fall into the comparison trap. And we know what it feels like. And we can help.

Allie says in her chapter to your daughter, "Your value doesn't come from how other people see you or from how you measure up to others. Your value comes from the fact that Jesus went to the cross for you."

**Comparison says:** Fix your eyes on the people around you.
**Culture says:** Fix your eyes on yourself.
**God says:** Fix your eyes on Jesus.

While comparison and culture seem to grab the victory many days, we can take steps to prepare our girls to meet the pull of comparison with maturity and strength. We can help them fix their eyes on Jesus as they recognize the source of their value and worth. So how do we do that? We said in chapter 2 that allowing our worth to be evaluated and determined by anyone but God inevitably leads to a sense of hopelessness. God's view of us is what matters. He made us. He knows us. He loves us. And he put an exclamation point on our extraordinary value by sending his own Son to die for us. But it's hard not to slip back into the habit of letting other people have a say. We live every day in a broken world, for goodness' sake. The tug is real! And it's *very real* for our daughters.

So let's talk about two practical and essential actions that set us up, and set our girls up, to break out of the trap of comparison. These two things are part of how we fix our eyes on Jesus instead of on ourselves or on others.

> **Celebrate** what God has given others, and leverage what God has given you.

## Celebrate What God Has Given Others

First, let's talk about *celebrating what God has given others*. It's a huge win for everyone when we get in the habit of replacing envy and jealousy with celebration and joy over another person's victories. Though it may not come naturally, we can develop the habit and let it become our default response. And before you know it, it will be authentic.

Pause reading for a second and ponder this: Is there a particular person whose victories or successes get under your skin? Do you find yourself diminishing their work or their achievements to make yourself feel better? Maybe you need to celebrate her success, or his success, proving that jealousy and envy are not your masters.

Because here's the thing: celebrating other people diminishes jealousy's power over you. And it will do the same for your girl. Imagine her having this skill going into high school, into college, and into adulthood!

When you celebrate, do it *out loud* and *on purpose*. Celebrating other people's successes spreads the joy around. Like us, our girls need to express their encouragement and congratulations toward another person *out loud*. This outward display of an inward decision often results in an unusual joy. Even if we don't feel like it on the front end.

35

Let's think for a minute about what celebrating others could look like. When you hear someone's good news and catch yourself immediately comparing, choose to celebrate instead:

- When your colleague gets a promotion, write a note of congratulations, even if you don't feel like it.
- When your neighbor down the street plans the incredible vacation you've been dreaming of, buy her a travel book or send her a link to a blog outlining fun activities to do there.
- When your daughter's friend makes the cheerleading squad, drive your girl to the store to grab a card or some balloons and deliver them.

It's amazing what happens in our hearts when we celebrate someone else's win. Celebrating them *out loud* and *on purpose* is a surefire way to avoid the trap of comparison. But celebrating another person is a choice. It takes some intentionality. It sometimes takes a bit of creativity. You might find it fun to brainstorm with your daughter about ways to celebrate the people around you.

After all, what's the alternative? Our girls can sulk in their own insecurity and envy others, leading to increased dissatisfaction and perhaps depression and anxiety. Or they can decide to rejoice in someone else's success, good fortune, and victories, in essence, clearing and cleaning the heart and experiencing more joy.

Celebrating others is a choice. It's intentional. It's better.

## Leverage What God Has Given You

And that brings us to the second practical and essential action. Contentment and peace also come as we learn to *leverage the gifts, talents, and opportunities God has given us.*

When we look around and compare, we are so focused on what

everybody else has that our appreciation for what God has given us is diminished. And we end up being poor stewards of those gifts. We might even miss out on amazing things he wants to do in us and through us.

Think about it this way: What you *have* is less important than what you *do* with what you have. So what are you going to do with what God has entrusted to you? Cute rhyme, huh? Say it again with a little sass. *What are you going to do with what God has entrusted to you?*

Jesus loved to speak in parables, and in the book of Matthew, he uses an interesting parable to drive home the point that what we do with what God has given us, what he has entrusted to us, is super important. When you have time, read the whole story in Matthew 25:14–30. And keep in mind that in almost all of Jesus's parables, someone represents God, and someone represents us. These parables helped to communicate to Jesus's followers what God is like.

For now, here's the gist of the parable. A man was going on a journey, and apparently he would be gone from his property and his assets for a long time. So he gathered three of his servants and made each of them responsible for certain amounts of his money according to their abilities. So they each started with different amounts. Fair? Maybe not, but it was the owner's decision to make.

Two of them invested what he gave them and increased the master's wealth. One of them dug a hole and buried the money. A long time passed, and the owner returned and asked them to account for how they stewarded the money. The owner was proud of the first two and put them in charge of even more. They had taken what was entrusted to them and made good use of it. But the music changes for the third servant. He basically told the master that because he feared him, he didn't take any chances and he buried the money. He didn't do anything with it. He basically buried it, ignored it, and moved on. He did nothing with the opportunity.

The master was unhappy. He pointed out that the servant not only didn't try to improve on what he was given but also was too lazy even to do the bare minimum. He could have at least put the money in the bank and made a little interest. So the owner took away what he'd given him and tossed him out. He wasn't a good steward of what the owner had entrusted to him.

Like the characters in Jesus's parable, we all are given different "amounts"—different gifts, different talents, different material assets, even different family dynamics.

- There will always be people who have more, and there will always be people who have less.
- There will always be someone prettier, and there will always be someone who wishes they looked like you.
- There will always be someone with a bigger or better house, and there will always be someone who wishes they had yours.
- There will always be someone who has a better or more desirable job, and there will always be someone who would love to have yours.
- There will always be someone who has more money, and there will always be someone who thinks your income would be all they'd ever need.
- There will always be someone whose child is smarter, or is a better athlete, or gets into a better school, and there will always be someone who wishes they had a child like yours.

But the interesting thing about the parable is that in the end, none of the servants were asked to give an account to another servant. And none of them were asked to comment on how well or poorly the other two stewarded what they were given. *They were required to give an account to the one who provided them with what they had to invest.*

And so it is with us. There is no need to look around. Even if others have more, God doesn't owe something *to* us. But he does require something *from* us. He requires us to take what we've been given, whether much or little, and steward it well. There will come a time when we give an account to him alone for how we handled what we were given. What are you doing with what God has given you?

So the two actions that set us up, and set our girls up, to break out of the comparison trap are to celebrate what God has given others and to leverage what God has given us. Even on days when we don't feel like we've been entrusted with much, we can pause and remind ourselves that we have.

A little chunk of verses in Ephesians 2 is my go-to when I need to increase my gratitude for the gifts God has given me. Several years ago I decided to memorize verses 4–10:

> **Because** of his great love for us, God, who is rich in mercy, made us alive with Christ even when we were dead in transgressions—it is by grace you have been saved. And God raised us up with Christ and seated us with him in the heavenly realms in Christ Jesus, in order that in the coming ages he might show the incomparable riches of his grace, expressed in his kindness to us in Christ Jesus. For it is by grace you have been saved, through faith—and this is not from yourselves, it is the gift of God—not by works, so that no one can boast. **(VV. 4–9)**

And then this next verse is an exclamation point that drives home the fact that God has a particular and perfect plan just for you. It's been planned for a long time. It's unique to you. And it's the core reason why you don't need to measure your story against anyone else's: "We are God's handiwork, created in Christ Jesus to do good works, which God prepared in advance for us to do" (v. 10). We are his handiwork. Isn't that incredible? That means he thoughtfully, intentionally, and carefully created us. After creating us, he didn't just toss us into the world to see how we'd fare. He created us in Christ Jesus to do specific works he planned just for us. He thought it through!

Another verse that reinforces the idea of God having a particular purpose for each person is from one of my all-time favorite psalms. It falls right smack in the middle of a pretty well-known psalm of David's. Psalm 139 speaks of God's extraordinary awareness of you and how thoughtfully and carefully he made you. Here's my favorite part: "All the days ordained for me were written in your book before one of them came to be" (v. 16). Not only did he make you, but he also knows every single one of your days, and he's known them always. Amazing!

Fast-forward to the New Testament. The writer of the book of Hebrews uses the metaphor of a race: "Let us run with perseverance the race marked out for us" (12:1). He implies that our race, our life map, was in place ahead of our arrival. God marked (past tense) it out.

I don't know about you, but this is so encouraging to me. The God who created the entire universe sees me. He knows me and prepared a work for me. And for you. And for your daughter.

God has *a plan, a race, a great work* for *you*. A way to leave behind a legacy that outlives you. And we don't want to miss leveraging that in a way that honors him, fulfills us, and models the way forward for our girls.

How has God uniquely gifted you?

What's something people are always saying you do well?

What do you wake up excited about?

Maybe you're a master of organization. Maybe you love leading or teaching. Perhaps God gave you a skill like building or baking or painting. Maybe you're a great listener or a great encourager or gifted at helping other people sort out their issues. Leverage those strengths.

Often we deflect compliments, but sometimes they can be a clue as to what we should be leveraging. How can you put your unique skills to good use? What wisdom could you offer others? What blessing is God asking you to steward and share?

Be inspired by others, and be motivated. At the end of the day, take your gifts, talents, and opportunities and leverage them the way God intended. Live *your* story. Don't glance to the left or to the right, comparing. Don't let other people's gifts steal your joy. Ultimately there is no win in comparison. But there is extraordinary satisfaction in waking up every day in the center of God's will for your life, being exactly where God wants you to be and doing exactly what he has called you to do.

So take your cue about your worth from the one who made you, the one who loves you, and the one who redeemed you by sending his Son, Jesus Christ. You are *that* valuable to him.

Again, Philippians 4:8 nails it: "Whatever is true, whatever is noble, whatever is right, whatever is pure, whatever is lovely, whatever is admirable—if anything is excellent or praiseworthy—think about such things."

Focusing on what's true, noble, right, pure, lovely, and admirable doesn't leave us much room for comparison. It renews our minds and resets our hearts. And we begin to be able to authentically celebrate other people's wins.

So to wrap up . . .

**Celebrate** the gifts, talents, and opportunities God has given others.

**Leverage** the gifts, talents, and opportunities God has given you.

If you celebrate what God has given others and leverage what God has given you, you will avoid the comparison trap. You will be free to live a life that brings God maximum glory, brings you maximum satisfaction, and offers your daughter an opportunity to see what that looks like.

Imagine *that* for your girl!

# CHAPTER 4

# Family Is Forever

In early fall 2019, an amazing guy named Clay Cooney proposed to Allie on a dock at a North Georgia mountain lake. It was beautiful and sweet and momentous. The sun was setting over the autumn-orange mountain, and the lake was a sparkling greenish blue. Immediately after the resounding "Yes!" from Allie, two pontoon boats across the lake cranked up, filled with screaming and cheering friends and siblings headed toward the newly engaged couple. There were happy tears and an unforgettable celebration. Barbecue was involved, and a lot of dessert. This mama loved every second.

Know what happened the minute that celebration ended? Know what this mom-of-the-bride catapulted into? You guessed it. Wedding planning. I'm a planner, so this was my jam.

First order of business: create a Google doc for keeping everything organized, and share it with the handful of people who would be making things happen. And then make lists. Make lists of lists. Make lists of things that need to be listed. And then live by lists. Wake up to lists. Go to bed thinking of tomorrow's list. That's what I did. For about six months, lists dictated my days. I was also finishing seminary and doing normal life too, so without lists I knew

I wouldn't make it. Okay, perhaps I'm being a tad dramatic. But I love lists, in case you didn't guess that.

Clay has a big family and a deep well of friends. He had a lot of folks on his invite list. Same for Allie. So the guest list was *long*, like, five-hundred-people long. We chose an outdoor venue, so there were tents and chairs and tables and even bathroom trailers to rent. We would need a lot of food and cake and flowers and sparkly lights and wedding favors. Oh, and dresses and tuxes for attendants and family. So much excitement for this wedding day coming up in early April—April 4, 2020.

Do you see where this is going?

Yep. You guessed it. Covid. The week before the wedding, rumor was that the governor was going to call for Georgians to "shelter in place" for two weeks. That would mean no wedding. So six days before the wedding, Allie called Andy and me and announced that she and Clay wanted to go ahead and get married. "Mom, like, today."

After a bit of speechless stammering, and simultaneously wrapping my head around the idea of accelerating everything from "a week from now" to "like, today," I begged Allie to give me twenty-four hours. "Just give me twenty-four hours. We can do this."

At this point in Covid world, citizens were being asked not to gather in large groups, which at that time were defined as any number over fifty. So we shot text messages to family and close friends and let them know to gather back at the proposal spot on the lake the following day. Then we composed the dreaded email to five hundred announcing the cancellation of an April 4 wedding.

With the help of a handful of family, a few dear friends, and Allie's and Clay's superstrong brothers, we pulled it off. The wedding was beautiful. We got most of the flowers from the local Trader Joe's. Our florist created a gorgeous last-minute bridal bouquet.

The cake vendor whipped up a smaller version of the planned cake. The photographer and videographer happened to be available that day. The musicians showed up with a scaled-down version of the band. And our favorite barbecue vendor saved the day with dinner for about thirty-seven people.

When the whole thing was over and Allie and I were having our final moment before she headed across the lake in the same pontoon boat that brought their friends over on proposal night, she looked at me with big tears about to spill down her cheeks and said, "Mom, it was perfect."

We had so much processing to do on the heels of all that chaos. There was loss, in some ways. There was a twinge of disappointment over foiled plans. But do you know what my main takeaway was? At the end of the day, the most important thing is relationships. The chaos calms down. The details pass away. The celebrations subside. But the relationships stay. *Family* is everything.

Here's something to think about:

**We're** only as happy as our core relationships are healthy. We're only as content as our core relationships are mutually satisfying.

We experience the truth of that even if we haven't thought it through before.

When our core people are sad, we're sad. When they celebrate, we're quick to celebrate too. And when something happens to cause a rift in a relationship with one of them, we can't just shake it off. It hangs on. It lingers. And we carry around the weight until we get it resolved. Broken relationships take a heavy toll on us. On our emotional health. On our mental health. It's worth it to do what we can to keep our relationships healthy. Why? Because we were created for relationships.

We talked in chapter 2 about being made in God's image. So much is wrapped up in that truth. If you do a deep dive into the book of Genesis, particularly the first chapter, you'll discover just that. God made us to image him structurally—in our purpose of ruling over creation, as he rules over everything. But throughout the pages of Scripture, and especially as we follow Jesus through the Gospels, we see that we are also to image him relationally.

God created us for relationship with himself. *And* he created us for deep and meaningful relationships with each other, once again, imaging him. In imaging him relationally, we reflect some of the most obvious attributes of God: he is loving (1 John 4:16), merciful (Ephesians 2:4), faithful (1 Thessalonians 5:24), good (Psalm 25:8), and just (Deuteronomy 32:4), to name a few.

At the core of who he made us to be is a deep need to be properly related to others.

You've probably lived long enough to recognize that we are all wired to be relational. When something great happens to us, we can't wait to call our person, or our people, to tell them. When something hard or disappointing happens, we need to find our person right away and unload a bit of our pain, leaning into their comfort and their encouragement. Even in the normalcy of life, we want our people, those with whom we can share the highs and lows at the end of the day. And because of that, we find ourselves in need of circles. Circles of family. Circles of friends.

For this chapter, let's focus for a few minutes on the inner circle of family. Our inner-circle people are the ones who matter most to us. They're the people God assigned to us. And usually, they're the people who are permanent in our lives. We get to pick our friends, but we don't typically get to pick our family members. Because of that, family relationships are unique. They're special. They can also sometimes be the hardest.

We more readily share the real us with the people closest to us, the ones who know us best. That's why it's so easy to allow our frustrations and even our anger to rain down on the people closest to us. They're often the safest and are going to love us anyway, at least for a while, right? Depending on the age of your daughter, you may or may not have experienced this very thing in your relationship with her.

Before starting our current church, Andy and I spent a bunch of years in youth ministry. There, we experienced an interesting phenomenon that typically happened more with girls than guys. Without meaning to, teenage girls often place their moms in the unique category of *humans without feelings*. Let me paint a real-life picture of it for you.

When I was twenty-six years old and pregnant with our first baby, I was a small group leader for tenth-grade girls at our church. I decided to take them to my grandparents' beach house on Hilton Head Island for their spring break. Let me pause and tell you a little detail that I believe is relevant to the story: I was told I was having a baby girl. Clearly, ultrasounds were not what they are now because I was pregnant with Andrew. He's a boy.

I ended up having a C-section but needed to be put to sleep because of a fever. The medical team didn't want to give an epidural to someone with a fever because of the increased risk of infection. That's pretty much all I know about medical things. And it's possible I'm not even remembering that correctly, but that's the way I tell the story. Bottom line: I was put to sleep believing I would wake up to a blonde-haired or bald-headed baby girl. But I awakened to a black-haired baby boy. I have a memory of coming out of anesthesia to Andy standing at my bedside with a light-blue bundle in his arms. "Sandra, we have a boy!"

It was super weird, and I slurred out that I needed proof there had not been a baby swap or a hospital mix-up. Thankfully, one of the nurses in the delivery room was a member of our church and promised me she saw this beautiful, dark-haired baby boy lifted from my own abdomen.

Could she be in on the conspiracy? Maybe. But as it turned out, the baby, who would have no name for a few days because we only had a girl name picked out, looked exactly like Andy's baby pictures. It all turned out fine. We're super fond of Andrew now.

Back to my illustration . . .

So there I was in Hilton Head with twelve tenth-grade girls and another leader a little older than I was who had a daughter of her own. We had a great time, worked on our tans, ate a lot of junk food, and talked about deep and meaningful things as we studied Scripture in the evenings. Other than a few "whale" jokes at the expense of my protruding belly, the girls were sweet and kind and fun and funny. Which is why what happened next was so jolting.

One of the girls called home to ask her mom a question. Because of proximity, not nosiness, I could hear the daughter's end of the conversation. Her tone of voice was nothing like the tone she used with me, or the other leader, or the other girls. She was snippy and rude and extremely impatient with her mom. When she wrapped up the call, I was standing nearby and commented about how rude she sounded with her mom. Her response was, "It was *just* my mom!" Translation: *Moms don't count. You can say whatever you want to them. They aren't in the same category as all other humans.*

Want to know what my seven-months-pregnant-with-what-I-thought-was-a-girl brain was thinking? "Oh, just your mom? You mean the one who carried you in her belly for nine months, risking her life for you? The one who threw up for three months but did her best to take that nasty prenatal vitamin anyway? The one who got a bunch of glossy stretch marks across her tummy and rear? The one who developed a big blue vein in her leg? *All for you!* That mom? Oh yeah, you're totally right, it's *just your mom.*"

Pardon the sarcasm. I jest. Kind of.

Fair or not, some version of this scenario often happens in mother-daughter relationships. Why? Because usually a mom is the safest and most consistent relationship in a daughter's life. She's possibly the only person a girl believes will love her 100 percent of the time, no matter what. She's the innermost person in the innermost circle of her teenage daughter. This very phenomenon might be partly why you're doing this book with your girl—either to help address a similar situation or to try to head it off at the pass.

I have some good news either way. The more we talk about our Philippians passage, the more you'll be set up for meaningful and honest conversations with your daughter and the more easily you'll be able to address situations similar to this one.

In Allie's chapter to your daughter, she acknowledges that in your daughter's season of life, a lot of things are outside her control. She didn't get to choose her family, and she has little control over the decisions they make. But there are some things she *can* control!

Allie talks about three things for your daughter to "dwell on," consider, and work toward as she navigates family relationships. These three things certainly apply to friendships and other relationships outside of family, but they're important to keep in the forefront of her brain when dealing with family dynamics. And they're important to keep in the forefront of our mom brains too. There's no age expiration on these.

They are appreciation, forgiveness, and gentleness.

Take a look at Philippians 4:5. This verse says simply, "Let your gentleness be evident to all." Paul continues a few verses later by delivering a list of things for us to dwell on, for us to train our minds to think about. These things will aid us in our endeavor to be gentle with others: "Whatever is true, whatever is noble, whatever is right, whatever is pure, whatever is lovely, whatever is admirable—if anything is excellent or praiseworthy—think about such things" (v. 8).

This list is not exhaustive. It's meant to get us thinking. We know this because of other verses Paul wrote throughout the thirteen books of the Bible attributed to him. In this Philippians passage, however, Paul emphasizes gentleness by giving it its own sentence. He's singling it out. I wonder if he does that because he knows that our attitude, especially in our close relationships—family relationships—often trends away from gentleness.

As I reflect on the gospel accounts of Jesus's life and inter-actions, I can't think of any encounters with individuals where he didn't exhibit gentleness. *Unless* they were mistreating people. When he was irritated with the Pharisees, it was because of the way they treated the people they were supposed to be leading (Matthew 23:4–13). When he was angry in the temple over money being exchanged and the buying and selling of sacrificial animals (Matthew 21:12–13; Mark 11:15–18), it was because people were being "robbed" and taken advantage of *in God's name* and *in God's temple*! Take cover if you do that. It doesn't go well.

So back to our three things.

## Appreciation

Allie presents for your daughter's consideration the idea of appre-ciating you. I know! Awesome, right? But that can certainly work both ways as we figure out how to be considerate and appreciative of our girls, especially as they navigate the ins and outs of hormone changes and all the potential tension that comes along with middle and high school drama.

Appreciation is an expression of gratitude. Around the Stanley house we tend to over-thank. Why? Because unexpressed grati-tude feels to others a lot like ingratitude. Be generous with your gratitude. Err on the side of over-thanking and over-appreciating people, especially family. Even for things they are *expected* to do.

Here's a little parenting gem for you. It's also a marriage gem. Actually, it's an every-relationship gem:

**What's** rewarded is repeated.

And gratitude is a simple reward to those around us. It says, "I see what you did and I appreciate it."

So thank your daughter for doing her homework, or making her bed, or taking out the trash. Even if it's for a chore on the refrigerator chart and she feels like she doesn't really have a choice, say thank you and mean it. Gratitude goes a long way in our relationships because words of gratitude are life-giving words. Catch your daughter doing good. Highlight it. Celebrate it. And thank her for it, even if you're not the direct recipient.

## Forgiveness

It's usually pretty easy for us to forgive our kids. We're the parent, and we love them fiercely. We have more context for life and more experience navigating hard situations. But forgiveness is still kind of new for our girls. They're finding their way and might be more affected by our unintended wounding. And dad wounds—those are tough on our girls. Here's the thing about that: your husband has never been a teenage girl before. I know, revolutionary thought. But it means he's going to get it wrong with your daughter and not even have a clue why what he said was the wrong thing to say. You might have to help out here—both with your husband's awareness and your daughter's patience! Allie addresses this in her chapter too.

If your daughter can begin to understand the power of forgiveness *now*, she will be so far ahead in the relational game when she finally launches from your home. Forgiving someone is emotional for sure. But it's transformational too. And it's the clearest picture of what following Jesus looks like.

Jesus took forgiveness to the next level, and he asks us to do the same. We're not just to forgive and walk away. We are to restore. Restoring a relationship is harder but so important. Mental forgiveness is only the first step. It's only half the equation. In our inner-circle relationships, our family relationships especially, we are to take the next step of restoring the broken relationship.

Think about this: The story of redemption is the story of how God *reconciled* his rebellious children (us) to himself. He was not content only to forgive. God's forgiveness was a means to an end. *Restoring* the broken relationship was, and is, his ultimate aim.

Jesus commanded us to do for others what he did for us: "In your relationships with one another, have the same mindset as Christ Jesus" (Philippians 2:5). What was his mindset? Remember the parable of the lost sheep? "Oh well. If that rogue sheep wants to rejoin the flock, he knows where to find us." No. The good shepherd left the ninety-nine sheep to go after the one that was lost. There's forgiveness and there's more. There's restoration.

Obviously, we have to talk with our girls about healthy versus unhealthy relationships. We have to talk about boundaries. We have to talk about safety. But in healthy relationships, especially inner-circle relationships, the right choice is almost always reconciliation.

Side note: With unhealthy friendships or relationships, the win is *having no regrets*. Sometimes reconciliation back to the way things were isn't the goal. But can we lay our heads on our pillows at night and know we've removed the relational obstacles that were ours to remove? That's part of forgiveness too.

Let's let our girls see us forgive and restore. Let's model it. And then encourage them to do the same.

## Gentleness

Ah, gentleness. It sounds so peaceful. Ethereal maybe. Let's just all be gentle with one another. Also, can we walk barefoot through a meadow wearing flowy dresses and maybe weave some sweet little flowers into our hair? Sounds nice. Sounds easy. But it's not.

I'm pretty sure I know the reason gentleness is on the list of the fruit of the Spirit in Galatians 5: "The fruit of the Spirit is love, joy, peace, patience, kindness, goodness, faithfulness, gentleness, self-control; against such things there is no law" (vv. 22–23 NASB). I think it's because being gentle is hard. In the busyness of life, and with the pace we're keeping, our default response to interruptions or the unkindness of others is anything but gentle. I'm a nice person, mostly, but I do have frequent nongentle private conversations in my head. Which likely reflect my heart. I've lived just long enough not to say these things out loud because it doesn't help anything. But not because I'm an inherently gentle person.

Thankfully, gentleness is something the Holy Spirit imparts to us when we lean in and allow him to live through us, communicate through us, respond through us. Even when we don't feel like it. It's kind of like a superpower. So next time someone asks what you'd pick if you could have a superpower, say, "Oh, I do have superpowers. Nine of them to be exact!"

In Allie's chapter to your daughter, she talks about being gentle and specifically addresses gentleness toward siblings. This might not be the case in your family, but in ours, sibling gentleness was rarely a thing. Quite the opposite. Once again, inner-circle people often bear the brunt of our mood swings and irritation. And siblings are prime candidates.

Just a quick encouragement to you. Now that I have adult children, one of my greatest and deepest joys is watching how much they love and appreciate each other. It literally brings tears to my eyes. I think it's another image-of-God thing. It brings such joy to God's heart when his children love and honor one another. And it brings such joy to our mama hearts too. So here's the encouragement part: There were days when our kids were growing up and all living at home when I thought they'd never end up liking each other at all, much less preferring and choosing each other, including each other in the details of their adult lives. Seeing their friendship now is awesome. And strong connections like these begin at home as we model gentleness for our kids and encourage gentleness among them.

How about a little practical help with that?

Help your daughter recognize her volatile times, her more vulnerable times, her mood swings, and her triggers. And practice appropriate responses. Remind her that real life happens. There will always be people who push her buttons. Just like there are people who still push yours.

The sooner your sweet girl learns to identify all of that and have a practiced approach for responding, including leaning into the Holy Spirit for help, the sooner gentleness will become her default. It's amazing to watch that happen. But don't pop the popcorn yet. You've got a little work to do first!

As we wrap up this chapter, I'd like to point out that appreciation, forgiveness, and gentleness are part of transitioning from a *me* mentality to a *we* mentality for your daughter. Babies are born 100 percent *me* focused. That's innate. That's natural. But as they grow and develop, they increasingly become part of a *we*, a family. They begin to understand the importance of their inner-circle people. And thriving in those relationships involves putting some selfishness aside. For the rest of their lives, they'll have to give up a little of *me* to be part of a healthy *we*. Why? Because ultimately there is no satisfying *me* without a *we*.

Again, we were created to be in relationships—with God and with the people around us.

As you talk through these three important ideas with your daughter—appreciation, forgiveness, and gentleness—wrap her in your arms and remind her how much you love being a *we* with her.

**CHAPTER 5**

# Finding Your People

Okay, moms, pretend with me for a moment . . .

You're headed to your daughter's room. You know it's a disaster because you were in there delivering a stack of clean clothes just before she got home from school. You rounded the corner and your soul died when you saw the mess. You couldn't see the floor for the discarded outfits she decided against when she was in a hurry to shoot out the door earlier. Also, a collection of glasses, plates, and bowls was hanging out in there having a crusty dish party even though you thought there was a house rule against food in bedrooms. Anyway, she's home now and you're bracing yourself for the "stop what you're doing and clean your room please" discussion.

I may or may not have had a similar—or this exact—situation occur in our house. Even so, when I think of parenting highlights, a memory of eighteen-year-old Allie in a setting not too unlike what I've just described rushes in. I rounded the previously mentioned corner that led to her room. Clothes were strewn about, and she was plopped on the floor in the middle of them. If it had been a Disney movie scene, the articles of clothing and dishes would've been live characters deep in conversation as they whispered their

57

conjectures about what she was so excitedly typing on her laptop. She had a seriously determined look on her face.

Knowing better than to interrupt, and remembering that the time to enjoy watching her sitting on the floor of her childhood room was drawing to a close, I simply took in the scene and basked in the beauty of this young woman who was nearly an adult. After a few seconds she looked up and said, "Mom, tell me what you think of this. These are Allie's Rules for High School. I'm giving them to my ninth graders."

To give you a little context, Allie served as an assistant small group leader to middle school girls on Sunday mornings at our church. In a couple of weeks, that group would enter Milton High School as freshmen. Allie had poured a lot of time and energy into these girls over their three years of middle school. And she adored them. Having just graduated from Milton High School herself, she had a fresh perspective on exactly what they'd be encountering over the next four years. She decided to put together a list of "guidelines" that she hoped would help them navigate the treacherous waters of high school.

As Allie read her list to me, I slowly made my way to the floor to sit beside her. By the time she reached the end of her list, my eyes were flooded with tears and I was overwhelmed and amazed at her maturity and strength.

I knew she had made good choices throughout high school and had navigated some hard situations in ways that demonstrated her love for Christ and desire to obey him. But to hear the "rubber meets the road" advice she put on paper was incredible. In that moment, I even loved her messy room.

So I'm going to share twenty of Allie's Rules for High School with you! Pass them on to any rising high schoolers you might know.

1. Surround yourself with people who build you up, not people who tear you down.
2. Treat your kisses like you have a limited supply.
3. Guard your heart. Seriously . . . your heart is precious.
4. Stay vertical. Set your physical boundaries and stick to them.
5. Have an accountability partner and be willing to tell HER everything.
6. Be so so so so so so so SO SO SO SO careful who you date.
7. If you're wondering if you should break up with him, break up with him.
8. If your girl gets broken up with, go buy her a stuffed animal, a blanket, candy, and lots and lots of ice cream. (Other gifts are acceptable too.)
9. Pray, PRAY, PRAY! Don't ever forget how much you need God.
10. Have a quiet time. It may seem like a hassle, but it will help you stay close to God.
11. Be nice to your parents. They love you and want the best for you, so if you disagree with them, just realize that they are a lot smarter than you . . . sorry about it.
12. If you find yourself lying to your parents or other adults in your life, backtrack and get out of that situation IMMEDIATELY. You are somewhere you do not want to be.
13. Never be afraid to say no. It's better to be a wimp than dead.
14. When you fall on your face, get back up and keep moving (literally and figuratively).
15. Journal so you can look back and see what God has done in your life.

16. Even when you don't want to, GO TO CHURCH!
17. If it's not classy, don't do it.
18. Don't judge. Even when people are doing things you don't agree with, show them love.
19. Pause before you speak . . . this will prevent a lot of problems.
20. Selfies are for faces.

Some of these are funny but true. Some are serious and also true. A few are warnings meant to keep the girls between the rails and to keep them safe. Most have to do with friendships and relationships. Why? Because the wrong friendships and relationships are the main areas that have the potential to take our girls down, delivering consequences and regret they'll have to carry for seasons to come. Allie had watched as some of the girls who orbited her high school world lugged around loads of regret they'd never anticipated. They thought the decisions they were making didn't really matter. But they did.

Not only are friendships and relationships the two areas with the highest potential for hurting your daughter; they're also the main culprits taking her attention away from you and the family. The struggle is real. Friendships and attraction become the focus. Boyfriends. Best friends. Frenemies. And it's hard. You're the one who labored to bring her into the world—and the one who continues to labor to ger her to the finish line of growing up. And yet when our girls hit about fourteen, they begin leaning into the advice and counsel of humans who have no more perspective and experience than they do. While it's frustrating, it's normal. That's why it's important to have the kind of mother-daughter relationship that allows you to have continual influence. And that's not impossible. It's why you're taking the time to read this book. It's why you do a lot of the things you do!

In Allie's chapter to your daughter, she breaks friendship and attraction into three stages of relationships: before you get close, while you are close, and when you are no longer close. And in all three stages, she emphasizes the importance of *loving well*. While there are similarities between relationships with friends and relationships with boys, there are certainly some differences. We'll touch on both as we discuss each stage.

Side note: These three stages apply to us moms too. I'll let you contextualize for yourself, but the adult version of these stages is helpful to think through. As we mature, hopefully the relationships in our lives stay relatively stable. But if we are constantly transitioning through all three stages—unless we physically move—the problematic common denominator might be us. Maybe we have some personal work to do. Sorry if that smashed your toes a little.

Let's break down these relationship stages.

## Before You Get Close

Starting brand-new relationships in middle school or high school can be tough, so it is a significant advantage when our kids already have some friendships in place. Maybe they connected and developed those relationships in elementary school or at church. One of the advantages to church student ministry is the carryover of those friendships at school. As soon as our kids enter a new school or new class, their eyes search for "their person" or "their people." Just like ours do. We all want to feel like we belong. So as you coach your daughter through the friendship-development waters, help her ask some clarifying questions:

What kind of friends do I want to have?
What are the characteristics of good friendships?
What makes a lifelong friend?

What causes friendships to be short term, and how do I avoid those?

Do I want to become more like this person?

Is this someone I'd like to introduce to my parents and my siblings?

With both friendships and romantic relationships, we want our girls to care for people the way God intends. The apostle Paul spells out how a loving person behaves in relationship with others. He gives us a picture of perfect love. It's the love God has for us—and the love we should strive to have for one another:

> **Love** is patient, love is kind. It does not envy, it does not boast, it is not proud. It does not dishonor others, it is not self-seeking, it is not easily angered, it keeps no record of wrongs. Love does not delight in evil but rejoices with the truth. It always protects, always trusts, always hopes, always perseveres.
>
> Love never fails. (1 CORINTHIANS 13:4–8)

Allie has your daughter read this passage and circle each characteristic of love. So maybe you should too! Grab a pen or highlighter. Or if you're like me and are an Enneagram 1, grab a pencil so you can erase and make it perfect and not have to buy another book and start over.

Look at what you've circled and imagine your daughter's friends or potential boyfriends demonstrating this package of behaviors toward her. If she sets the bar high for the way she expects to be treated by a potential lifelong friend or spouse, that's a big win. And imagine if these characteristics become true of the way she treats the people around her. Including you. Including her siblings. That's a big win too!

Take a second look at the 1 Corinthians passage, then underline any characteristics you think you lack. Do a handful of them need some work? Your daughter will be thinking through the same thing, and I bet you two can have some great conversations as you honestly talk through some of them.

As Andy says in *The New Rules for Love, Sex, and Dating*, "Become the person the person you're looking for is looking for."[3] You might have to read that a couple of times to get it. But basically, become the kind of person that a potential great friend or great spouse would be attracted to. What kind of person are you looking for? Are *you* that kind of person?

Do you want relationships with people who are patient and kind, not envious or boastful or proud, who honor others and aren't self-seeking, who aren't easily angered and don't rehearse the wrong things you've done? Those who are truthful, who want to protect, trust, and hang in there even when times are hard? If so, then that's exactly who you should strive to be.

Also in *The New Rules for Love, Sex, and Dating*, Andy says this: "I'm absolutely convinced people who are committed to becoming the right people are better equipped to identify and avoid the wrong people along the way."[4]

## While You Are Close

Remember when you were your daughter's age and you found a new friend? Someone you connected with, had things in common with, and whose company you always enjoyed? Holly Harbin was that friend for me. We didn't know each other well until high school. And from ninth grade all the way to twelfth, we were inseparable.

A few things about Holly: Holly loved Jesus. Holly loved her family. And Holly was hilarious. Holly was a friend who always made me want to be a better version of myself. Not because she was judgy or demanding but because she was inspiring. She believed the best about people. She gave people the benefit of the doubt. But she wasn't afraid to walk away from relationships that weren't healthy or that had the potential to pull her down. When I think about high school, I see her as a gift God gave me—for the accountability and the encouragement to make God-honoring decisions. I hope you had a friend like that. If not, then I hope you do now. And I pray your daughter finds one too. Everyone needs a Holly.

Let's talk about what happens when your girl does find a best friend or a boy she's interested in. She's building that relationship. They're spending time together and getting to know each other better. She's lucky to have you paying attention and being willing to coach her through! Here are a few guiding principles to help your daughter in relationship situations she might face. Think these through and maybe chat with her about them later.

## Don't Trade What You Want Most for What You Want in the Moment

In friendships, but even more in dating relationships, it's easy to let what we want in the moment undermine what we truly desire for our future.

### EXAMPLES

Someday I hope to have a good story to tell my future husband about how I handled my dating life growing up. But the person I'm in a relationship with now is asking me to compromise in areas that could derail that story.

Bad trade!

---

Honesty is important to me. I hope to always be known as an honest person. But my good friend is encouraging me to hang out instead of studying for the upcoming test, and she's suggesting I cheat. She says everyone else does, so why shouldn't I?

Bad trade!

------

Kindness is important to me. I want people to see Jesus in me by the way I act. But someone is making fun of the kid in class who has a hard time with social awkwardness, and if I don't laugh, I'll probably be the next one made fun of.

Bad trade!

Don't trade what you want *most* for what you want *in the moment*. For your daughter, and for you, regret is always on the other side of those bad trades.

## Don't Let Your Future Be Negatively Influenced by People Who Won't Even Be in Your Future

The truth is, some people are only in our lives temporarily. Remember all those folks in your graduating class? How many do you still have a relationship with? Facebook friends don't count. So when your daughter moves on from middle school or high school, many of those people she will never see again. They won't be in her future.

The friends we hang on to are the like-minded ones who make us want to be better. Like Holly. That's why Solomon, the wisest man ever to live, besides Jesus, wrote proverb after proverb about wisdom and wise people. Listen to this one: "One who walks with wise people will be wise, but a companion of fools will suffer harm" (Proverbs 13:20 NASB).

When it comes to dating relationships, remind your precious girl what it looks like to be a Jesus follower as it relates to her sexuality. Allie isn't sharing this part in her chapter since we don't know the age of your daughter. But if she's old enough, the following three guidelines are great to talk about in an age-appropriate way:

> **Honor God with your body.** The Holy Spirit lives in you (1 Corinthians 3:16). You image your Father with your physical body (Genesis 1:27). Always honor God with your body, and by default you will honor other people's bodies too (1 Corinthians 6:20).
>
> **Don't be mastered by anything.** You already have a master. You have a heavenly Father who adores you and values you and treasures you, and it breaks his heart when you hurt yourself. When you let him be your master, there is no room to be mastered by pornography or addictions or even other people. Your Father knows exactly what's best for you, and he will provide for your every need.
>
> **Don't sexualize any relationship outside of marriage.** Sex outside of marriage sets us up for the temptation to be dishonest later or to lose the story we hope to tell someday. And it makes our lives much more complicated. Our good heavenly Father knows that and doesn't want that for us.

## When You're No Longer Close

There's probably no better time to let the counsel of Philippians 4:5, "Let your gentleness be evident to all," sink into our hearts and minds than when a relationship hits a bump or ends.

Allie says this to your daughter in her chapter: "The call to love people does not break down even if we break up." The admonition to love people and be gentle in our responses and attitudes toward them doesn't go away after someone hurts us or leaves us or fades out of our life. We are still called to *love well*.

Charlene, a mentor of mine, said something that has always stuck with me. When I was navigating the end of what had once been an important relationship to me, she said, "Sandra, the reality of life is that friendships phase in and phase out in different seasons of life. You need to determine which ones you want to be permanent and which ones are for a season." Char was right. There is an ebb and flow to relationships. And sometimes we simply have to open our hands and let them go.

When we move on from a friendship or a dating relationship, our gentleness and love should remain. Our responses, even when it's a messy breakup, are still to be Christlike. We're Jesus followers after all! If love is to characterize us, even our breakups should look something like the love passage in 1 Corinthians 13. We should exhibit patience and kindness. We shouldn't be envious and begrudging when good things happen to that person. We should make sure our words about that person are honoring, not selfish, not coming from anger, and not rehearsing to other people all the things they did wrong. That's love. That's how a Jesus follower responds, even when mistreated.

Two favorite verses come to mind that have to do with this very thing:

> **Be** kind and compassionate to one another, forgiving each other, just as in Christ God forgave you. **(EPHESIANS 4:32)**

> **Live** in peace with each other. And we urge you, brothers and sisters . . . be patient with everyone. Make sure that nobody pays back wrong for wrong, but always strive to do what is good for each other and for everyone else.
> **(1 THESSALONIANS 5:13–15)**

We can, and should, help our girls understand boundaries and appropriate separation, especially from unhealthy relationships. But coaching them to love well, even when dealing with a hard-to-love person, is a win for our girls. And it's amazing training for navigating the inevitable hard relationships in her future.

To wrap up, here are a couple of important reminders that apply to all three stages of relationships.

*Kindness* is for every person in every season. Even when we need to distance ourselves physically, our words about others can still be kind. Kindness sees people who feel invisible. Kindness includes those who are alone. Kindness serves those in need. Sometimes kindness simply listens to someone who needs to be heard. I love the way Andy sometimes talks about kindness in his sermons: "Kindness is loaning someone your strength instead of reminding them of their weakness."

*Compassion* is one of the characteristics Jesus modeled most for us. He modeled it when he saw someone hurting (John 8:1–11). He modeled it with people who were grieving (John 11:35). He modeled it with the crowds of people who were in need (Mark 6:34). He perpetually had compassion for people.

Compassion is different from sympathy. Sympathy and pity are shown through "feeling bad" for someone while we are glad we're not going through what they are. But compassion is sympathy *in action*. We see someone hurting or in need and we're moved to action. Often compassion is inconvenient. We're busy people after all. Compassion compels us to pause what we're doing, evaluate a situation, and figure out how we can help. It might cost us money, time, or convenience. It will likely cost us all three.

I might be stating the obvious, but doing hard relationships with kindness and compassion is not normal. It's especially not normal for middle school and high school breakups and friendship divisions. Because of that, if our girls handle bumpy relationships this way, people will take notice. Consider the following verse: "By this everyone will know that you are my disciples, if you love one another" (John 13:35). I love the way Chuck Swindoll says it: "It is the difference that makes the difference."⁵ The people around your girl will see that even during a hard breakup or a rift in a friendship, she is kind and compassionate. She knows how to forgive and move on.

Andy's sister, Becky, was a girl like that. I ran into a stranger in a store one day. She introduced herself and told me she had gone to high school with Becky. She said that all through high school Becky was quiet and tended to keep to herself. But she always noticed that Becky was kind. No matter what was thrown her way, she was kind in her response. This full-grown woman remembered, from decades earlier, a kind girl at school. Becky's kindness stood out. It made an unforgettable impact for good. It made this woman want to be a better person even though she and Becky weren't close friends.

It is the difference that makes the difference.

So let's revisit our verse:

**Love** is patient, love is kind. It does not envy, it does not boast, it is not proud. It does not dishonor others, it is not self-seeking, it is not easily angered, it keeps no record of wrongs. Love does not delight in evil but rejoices with the truth. It always protects, always trusts, always hopes, always perseveres.

Love never fails. **(1 CORINTHIANS 13:4–8)**

Love won't fail you. And love won't fail your daughter.

# CHAPTER 6

# Fear Is *Not* in Charge

Scary movies are *not* for me. I've never liked them. I've never understood how *anyone* can like them. In fact, I question the sanity of people who love scary movies. In my mind, there's something seriously wrong with people who choose to scare themselves—and even pay money to do it. Call me crazy . . .

When I was in ninth grade, some friends and I went to the neighborhood video rental store and came home with *The Amityville Horror*. Even though it would be my first horror movie, I already knew I was going to hate it. But I was in the minority, and my wimpy suggestion of *The Black Stallion* was decidedly shot down. We settled in a friend's basement with sleeping bags, Milk Duds, and microwave popcorn. I'm pretty sure I had a sweat mustache before the movie even started. My fears were not misplaced. The movie scarred me. *Scarred*, not scared. I slept on the floor in my parents' bedroom for several nights afterward, and my mom said I could never watch another movie like that. I did *not* need that stated restriction. I was done forever.

Decades later, as a full-grown adult mother, and now grandmother, if I wake up at 3:14 a.m., I shudder and squeeze my eyes tightly. I don't get up to grab a drink of water or use the restroom until it's 3:16 and the real threat has passed. If you haven't seen the movie, I'm so happy that you're free to head to the bathroom any time of the night. Yay you!

Unlike irrational fears from scary movies, some fears are valid. There are things in the world to be afraid of, no doubt. I could start listing them, but that might cause an unnecessary heart-rate spike when you're just here trying to love your daughter better.

Phobias are kind of funny though, as long as they're not yours. I hate snakes and anything that's slimy like a snake. As a kid, my older sister used to chase me with a purple plastic fishing worm. It was terrifying. She thought it was hilarious—until one day when she and I both discovered that her little sis had a mean left hook. Oh yeah. No more worm torture.

Fears can *cause* us to do things, eliciting emotional and even physical responses at times. Our bodies were created with an automatic fight-or-flight response to preserve our lives. You have something called a sympathetic nervous system that activates in response to dangerous or stressful situations. It increases your heart rate. It sends more blood or oxygen to areas of your body that need to engage. It responds in all kinds of ways to help you get out of danger. So in that way, fear can be helpful. Actually, it can be life-saving.

But fears can also harm us and *keep us* from doing things, trying things, stretching ourselves. Fear can be paralyzing at times. One of the most universal fears is the fear of public speaking. According to researchers, 77 percent of people fear public speaking. This fear is so significant it even has its own name: glossophobia. That's fun to say. "Glossophobia is the most commonly held situational fear."[6]

I think it's a valid fear. Probably because I used to have it. I've gotten used to public speaking, but I used to break out in a sweat, my heart would beat superfast, and my voice would feel shaky. I was sure I would trip going up the steps to the stage and for sure lose my train of thought in the middle of my talk. The more I experienced those things *not* happening, the more comfortable I got. But then I saw an actress trip going up the steps to receive her Academy Award, and that set me back. It took some time. But I'm good now.

Another danger of fear is that it can cause us to lash out in anger or lie to avoid punishment, embarrassment, or failure. Fear sometimes compels us to keep secrets or be dishonest. And for the record, secrets are almost always a bad idea because they lead to dishonesty, lying, and covering up. And the stress that comes on the heels of secrets isn't worth it. Trying to remember who knows what, and what's already been revealed, is too much. Besides, we're not meant to relate to one another that way.

At the root of most of our fears—the ones that aren't about getting away from true danger and preserving our literal lives—is a festering distrust of God. It's a distrust of God's *love* for us, his *provision* for us, and his *plans* for us.

And while we all struggle with fear at various levels, it doesn't have to be the boss of us. And it doesn't have to the be the boss of your daughter. Here are some bossy fears that may lead us to question God's love, provision, and plans for us:

- the fear of missing out
- the fear of being abandoned or left out
- the fear of disappointing people
- the fear of failing
- the fear of what other people will think of us

In Tindell Baldwin's book, *Popular*, she tells the heartbreaking story of her journey through her high school years as she was filled with hidden fears. Fears of missing out on what seemed most important at the time—being popular, being accepted, gaining attention, and being included. Fears of not being *the best* and not measuring up to her brothers, who seemed perfect. Those fears drove her to make decisions that wreaked havoc in her life and took time to heal and recover from.

Tindell is a friend of mine. She's a beautiful wife and mom, and she leverages her story any chance she gets as she disciples high school girls and encourages them not to let their fears be the boss of them.

I know you. You're like me. And you're having these conversations and reading this book to help your daughter recognize her fears and avoid the ensnaring traps set by those fears. But isn't it interesting how, if we're honest, we don't really outgrow this list of fears? While they might look a little different for us, at the core they're the same. Even when we've matured spiritually, emotionally, and age-wise, these fears always seem to swing back around in one form or another to undermine our trust in God. Sometimes they get the best of us. But, hopefully, increasingly they don't.

The good thing about talking with your daughter about fear is that you can truly relate. You can probably think of story after story of allowing fear to get the best of you throughout various seasons of your life. And talking about that with your daughter might unlock something in her and propel her to look fear in the face and process it with you—her safest person.

Speaking of safe people . . .

We've probably all witnessed the timid-child scenario. The one where a mom or dad is talking with someone unfamiliar to their toddler or young child. Maybe the parent is trying to introduce the child to someone he or she hasn't met before. The child scoots back behind the parent's legs and peeks around with uncertainty. Honestly, it got on my nerves when my kids did this. I wanted them to be brave and confident. What I learned is that courage and confidence build over time, and when a young child is fearful, it's normal for them to take a position of perceived safety behind their parent. They eventually come out once they feel it's safe, but only because of the *nearness* of the parent.

Here's another one. It might hit closer to home. You're sitting in a doctor's office waiting on the specialist. Because you're a normal human, uncertainty swirls in your mind and heart about a health situation you're facing. While you wait, all kinds of scenarios play out in your mind. But then the doctor walks in—the one who knows the most about your illness, the one who sees and treats similar patients all day long, five days a week. And you realize you're in good hands. And the fear dissipates a little because the knowledgeable doctor is *near*.

The nearness of a parent brings a feeling of safety to a child. The nearness of a great doctor delivers comfort and encouragement to a sick patient. And the nearness of our heavenly Father can do the same thing for us in the midst of our fears.

Look at this simple four-word sentence that's found in our Philippians passage: "The Lord is near" (Philippians 4:5).

This might sound a little crazy, but humor me. Say it out loud four times, each time emphasizing a different word:

*The* Lord is near.
The *Lord* is near.
The Lord *is* near.
The Lord is *near*.

If we let the truth of these four words penetrate our minds and hearts when fear abounds, it changes everything. Why? Because he is the powerful God whose presence *with us* brings peace.

Trust is the antidote to fear. We can trust that God does indeed love us. That he will indeed provide for us. And that he does indeed have plans for us that are fulfilling and good. Let's break it down.

## We Can Trust That God Loves Us

Even if you've spent a lot of time and energy running from God, or toward things counter to what a Jesus follower should pursue, he loves you and wants to have a relationship with you—one that's real, where you experience his nearness.

While we are unable to love perfectly, he is able. We looked at this in the previous chapter, but it's worth reviewing in the context of our fears. Through the apostle Paul, God tells us what real love looks like:

> **Love** is patient, love is kind. It does not envy, it does not boast, it is not proud. It does not dishonor others, it is not self-seeking, it is not easily angered, it keeps no record of wrongs. Love does not delight in evil but rejoices with the truth. It always protects, always trusts, always hopes, always perseveres.
>
> Love never fails. **(1 CORINTHIANS 13:4–8)**

That's the kind of love our heavenly Father has for us. A love that demonstrates patience. A love that models kindness. A love that isn't centered on self. A love that isn't puffed up with pride and arrogance. A love that honors. A love that is generous. A love that doesn't get angry and lash out. A love that chooses not to hold on to our misdeeds. A love that protects us and fights for us. A love that believes in us. And a love that stays *near*.

And God didn't just tell us what love looks like. He showed us. Jesus modeled for us what love looks like. He showed us how to treat people. He sacrificed his own comfort over and over. And then . . . the big one. Our heavenly Father showed his love for us by implementing an extraordinary plan to redeem us and save us through the death and resurrection of Jesus. He pulled us up out of the pit of our sin and shame, forgiving us and restoring us. *That's* love.

## We Can Trust That God Provides for Us

God's provision doesn't usually come packaged the way we expect, or even the way we might prefer. Often it's not until long after a situation resolves that we are able to see that *his* way and *his* timing were much better than what we had hoped.

Most of you reading this book probably don't often wonder whether you'll have your basic physical needs met—food, clothing, and shelter. But you certainly have *felt needs*, right? Both you and your daughter desire meaningful relationships (friendships, dating or marriage relationships, relationships with people who love and care for you). You both want to succeed at the activities you undertake (work, school, hobbies, sports). And you both likely want your lives to matter and have purpose.

Check out this verse that comes a little later in Philippians 4: "My God will meet all your needs according to the riches of his glory in Christ Jesus" (v. 19). Paul has just commended the people in the church at Philippi for their generosity in helping spread the gospel by way of their giving. And he reminds them that they don't need to worry, just like he isn't worried, because God sees their needs and will meet those needs. He can be trusted to provide.

And here's a favorite of mine when I need a reminder not to fear but instead to trust in God's nearness and provision for me. David wrote it:

> **The** Lord is my shepherd, I lack nothing.
>> He makes me lie down in green pastures,
> he leads me beside quiet waters,
>> he refreshes my soul.

> He guides me along the right paths
> > for his name's sake.
> Even though I walk
> > through the darkest valley,
> I will fear no evil,
> > for you are with me;
> your rod and your staff,
> > they comfort me. **(PSALM 23:1–4)**

The kid who became the most famous king of Israel was a shepherd boy first. He knew all about taking care of sheep, providing for their needs, and protecting them. He stayed near them. He made sure their physical needs were met. And he made sure his sheep were safe from lurking predators like wild animals and thieves. David saw God as his shepherd and as ours. Just as a shepherd does for his sheep, God provides for, guides, refreshes, and protects us. He stays near. We can lay down our fears, lean in, and trust him. When we do that, we lack nothing.

## We Can Trust That God Has Good Plans for Us

God is able to bless you abundantly, so that in all things at all times, having all that you need, you will abound in every good work. (2 Corinthians 9:8)

We are God's handiwork, created in Christ Jesus to do good works, which God prepared in advance for us to do. (Ephesians 2:10)

In chapter 3, about comparison, we talked about the fact that you and your sweet girl are God's handiwork. Other Bible versions interpret the Greek word Paul used as "workmanship." He created you and your daughter with intention—intention for what you'd do with your lives. He created you *with* purpose and *for* a purpose. Isn't that amazing? The God who created the world and everything in it created you intentionally. He created your daughter intentionally. And with purpose.

And in chapter 2 we talked about our identity being in Christ. God gave us our identity, our value, and our worth. But too often we pursue purpose with the intention of finding our identity in that instead. We're tempted to search for purpose in order to be more valuable and wanted and desired. We naturally lean toward *what we do* to define us—our purpose gives us our identity. But God wants it to be the other way around. *Our identity in him should be where we find our purpose.* We are made in the image of God. We are to image him to the world. That's our purpose! Jesus made it clear how to do that when he declared the two most important commandments: "'Love the Lord your God with all your heart and with all your soul and with all your mind.' This is the first and greatest commandment. And the second is like it: 'Love your neighbor as yourself'" (Matthew 22:37–39).

So how do we find the purpose for which he created us? How do we not miss the purpose he promised? I love the way John Burke says it in his book *Imagine Heaven*: "How do we know our unique purpose? It always starts with loving and seeking God, then following His lead to love the people closest to us, and then using the gifts and passions He's put in us to serve humanity."[7]

In Christ, we have purpose. One that is richer and deeper and better than anything we can dream up on our own. It's a gift and a promise from God. And he had it planned long before we were even born!

So what are you afraid of? What is your daughter afraid of? What driving fear takes your eyes off your Father in heaven and causes you to forget that he loves you, will provide for you, and has an amazing purpose for you?

Sometimes simply exposing the fear, admitting the fear, and being aware of the fear loosens its grip. Here are some questions to consider:

- Are you afraid of missing out?
- Are you afraid of being abandoned or left out?
- Are you afraid of disappointing people?
- Are you afraid of failing?
- Are you afraid of what other people will think of you?

Take a moment to identify your fears so you'll be ready to discuss them with your daughter. And then choose to believe that what God says is true *is actually true*. Viewing what scares us through the lens of our faith puts our faith into action and fights fear with truth. Your heavenly Father loves you. He will provide for you. And he has good plans for you.

One of my favorite devotional books says this: "Unbelief looks at God through the circumstances, just as we often see the sun dimmed by clouds or smoke. But faith puts God between itself and its circumstances, and looks at them through Him."[8] When fear tries to boss you around, remember that the Lord is near. And when you're weak, know that he is strong in you and through you and for you.

# CHAPTER 7

# Peace in the Chaos

I had my first panic attack in my late forties. Andy and I were in California for a conference, and we had a few hours free. We decided to do a little shopping. And by we, I mean I. I decided we'd do a little shopping. Andy needed socks. He suggested Target or Walmart. I googled Nordstrom. That's how it goes around here.

We arrived at Nordstrom and immediately went separate ways. He headed to the socks and conquered the socks. I headed to . . . everywhere. Browsing. Looking. Appreciating. I bumped into a cute tunic dress that screamed to be tried on. I don't love trying on clothes. But it looked worth it. So I headed to the fitting room with this potential treasure. I got to my little square of fitting-room space and undressed. I then proceeded to wrestle my way into this tunic dress. Elbows bumped the walls, and I even started to sweat a little bit. It was an over-the-head situation because there were no zippers or buttons or anything to open it up for entry. It was straight and narrow, as tunics are. But I was determined.

A little info about my paternally inherited shape: I'm on the tall and thin side, but I have wide shoulders. My height camouflages how wide they are. Even so, I managed to get that tunic over my head and shimmied down to its full length just above my knees.

As I peered in the mirror, I could see it was a quick and easy *no*. It didn't look good on me at all. So I immediately reversed the previous process and tried to remove the dress. It was so tight across the shoulders and back that I couldn't even position my arms and hands to begin getting out of it.

As I mentioned, I was already sweating a bit. And then my brain started shooting me messages. *You're stuck. You're trapped. There's no way to get out of this. This is your forever outfit.* My heart began beating hard. I started sweating even more. I was seriously trapped in that tunic. In my irrationality, I threw open the fitting room door and ran up the little hallway into the retail space. *Scissors. I have to find scissors.* Thankfully few people were in the store at that time of day and the salesperson was nowhere to be seen. A quick glance at the $200 price tag convinced me that scissors were not the answer. I guess I had regained a tad of rationality.

I took some deep breaths and went back to the fitting room. I started talking to myself out loud: "Sandra, you got into this tunic, and that means you can get out of it. You can do this. Deep breaths, girl. You've got this."

My heart was still pounding. I was still sweating and panicky. But I'm proud to say I eventually got out of it without scissors. I pulled the dress up as high as I could get it, then doubled over paper clip–style and shimmied out.

I got dressed in my own fabulously loose-fitting clothes and made my way out of the dressing room, smiling nervously and smoothing my hair. Casual, cool, calm . . . nothing to see here.

I found Andy in the men's sock section, and he immediately knew something was off. I provided a brief explanation of what had happened and let him know I'd be waiting outside gulping in the fresh air and freedom.

That was the first of several panic attacks for me. Apparently after you have one, you're prone to having them again. I learned that my best defense when that panicky feeling begins taking charge is to quote Scripture verses I have memorized. I always do my hard one (Ephesians 2:4–10) because I have to really concentrate on it. And it works every time. It's been a long time now since I've had a full-blown panic attack.

I know this isn't funny for people who've experienced panic attacks. And I hope this little story didn't initiate one for anybody. But my situation was a tiny bit hilarious. Especially when I later discovered that some Nordstrom fitting room areas are monitored. By live people. I don't know if that one was. But I can envision the security person calling over everyone within earshot to watch the crazy sweating lady do the tunic shimmy.

Enough of that though. I don't know a lot about actual anxiety and depression, which are often manifested in panic attacks and other outward expressions. But I do know that statistics show anxiety is on the rise and has become more prevalent in our nation.

It seems like every generation looks at the one coming behind it and says something along the lines of, "What's this world coming to?" Whether it's fashion choices, entertainment trends, music styles and lyrics, or the particular look of popular actors and artists, something always brings a sigh and a wish for the good ol' days. I find myself in that category now, and I don't like it one bit. I want to be forever young and cool. But, alas, what *is* this world coming to? Cue eye roll from our girls!

The truth is, it's probably just fine, this world of ours. Pendulums are always swinging, and changes are always happening. While there's no need for real panic, maybe we have a little work to do. There are some statistics we can't ignore as we raise these amazing girls God has given us. According to the National Institutes of Health, nearly one in three of all thirteen- to eighteen-year-olds experience an anxiety disorder.[9] Allie and I aren't licensed counselors, so we'll leave true anxiety counseling to them. But the lifestyle stresses and pressures our girls face daily are worth our discussion. These are often the basis, or the catalyst, for more significant anxiety issues later.

Think for a minute about what your middle school and high school experience was like: the rhythm of your day, your activities and schedule, your communication and interactions with friends. Remember house phones? Your friends had to *be home* for you to call and talk to them. Crazy times. Okay, do you have the picture of your teen years in mind? Now think of your daughter's. There's likely a huge difference.

Getting into college is harder than it's ever been. Our girls feel like their résumés have to be more robust than everyone else's just to get a second look from their school of choice. Your daughter's schedule is likely jam-packed with all the extracurricular activities she does, places she volunteers, and clubs she leads to help make her résumé stand out. If social media is a part of her everyday life, friend pressure and comparison are on another level. You can walk into any restaurant or shopping area and see kids striking poses for their next post, doing all they can to make their lives look polished and perfect. As soon as the picture snaps, the smiles disappear and are replaced by looks of serious contemplation as they edit the picture, write the caption, and publish the post. And then there's communication. Your daughter is in constant communication with her friends through texts, direct messages, and FaceTime. There's not much quiet in her life.

It's hard. Your girl is carrying a lot. Throw some hormone spikes and skews into the mix and it's no wonder you're sometimes left standing in the kitchen wondering what heinous crime she crafted from your simple "Would you like a sandwich?" And honestly, our adult lives are way more packed and stressful than our moms' were when they were raising us, right? What has ramped up for our girls ramped up for us too.

In the chaotic everyday pace of attending meetings, going to events, meeting obligations, carpooling kids, caring for parents, serving others, finding time to work out, running errands, making sure our people have food, and checking in on social media so we're up to date with who's doing what, we're running ourselves ragged. Even typing that sentence kind of wore me out.

But there's hope. There's hope for us, and there's hope for our girls. Even though you're busy, your daughter has *you*. And you're taking all the steps you can to help her develop and build a faith that will serve her *in* and *after* these stressful teen years. So keep reading, because help is on the way! God has made some amazing promises that address the emotions and stresses of busy lives. He promises to cut through the commotion and chaos and deliver . . . wait for it . . . *peace*.

Ah, peace. Even the word is like a deep breath. Let's look at our Philippians passage once again. This part is so good! Ready?

> **Do** not be anxious about anything, but in every situation, by prayer and petition, with thanksgiving, present your requests to God. And the peace of God, which transcends all understanding, will guard your hearts and your minds in Christ Jesus. **(4:6–7)**

There's a lot to unpack in this incredible passage. And it's connected to a promise. Let's break it down.

"Do not be anxious about anything" (v. 6). We touched on this in chapter 2, on identity. *Yeah, right. I'll just not be anxious or worried about anything. No problem.*

- My big presentation coming up at work? Not a problem. It's just for the CEO. No worries.
- My daughter taking the SAT? Just chillin' over here, drinking coffee. Not anxious for her at all.

- Awaiting a call back with my mammogram results? Not gonna fret. Hey, let's go dancing!

Obviously, those responses are nowhere near realistic. And they are far from the goal. Paul's instruction not to be anxious isn't about pretending nothing stressful is going on. It's not about putting our heads in the sand or ignoring scary stuff. He gives us further instruction when we keep reading. "But in every situation, by prayer and petition, with thanksgiving, present your requests to God" (v. 6). There it is. There's how we actually do it.

An adverse situation arises. My knee-jerk response is to worry. Or to fret. Or to feel anxious. Or even to get angry. How do I respond? Maybe I text my husband and unload all my angst. I tell him how mad I am at my boss or coworker or the mean, nosy neighbor. Maybe I call my sister or my mom or my best friend. I tell them all about it. I let them vent with me or give me some advice. Those responses are options. Maybe not even bad ones.

But what does Paul suggest? Paul tells us that the way of Jesus is a different approach. First, find a quiet spot away from everyone. Get on your knees and tell God all about your situation. Open your hands. Open your heart. Spill it all out and tell him what you hope for. But while you do, lace it all with thanksgiving, like this:

- Thank him for allowing you to come to him.
- Thank him for any blessings associated with this hardship.
- Thank him for what he's going to do, whether it's soon or whether it's later.
- Thank him whether you can see his answer or not.
- Thank him for his promise that he is *with you* in this tough time.
- And thank him for the lessons you'll learn in the process.

Prayer and petition, laced with thanksgiving, is a beautiful way to express surrender to God. And surrender is important. It announces our trust. It acknowledges that God sees what is impossible for us to see. He sees the past, present, and future all at once. His perspective is bigger, and his plan will be better.

When we surrender, we say to him, "Father, your ways are better and higher and way more informed than mine. Thank you for this opportunity. *Help me do what I can do and to leave the rest to you.*"

What do you get in return? "The peace of God, which transcends all understanding, will guard your hearts and your minds in Christ Jesus" (Philippians 4:7). Peace. He promises peace. Isn't that what we all really need? We've lived long enough to know life can be hard. Some days are harder than others. And on those days, peace is what we need.

That's exactly what he promises, because he knows that's exactly what we need. God is bigger than any problems that come our way. He is sovereign and in control of everything. And he offers us peace. In the midst of the storms, he offers peace. In the face of danger, he offers peace. Even in the busyness and chaos of life, he offers peace. And get this. His peace *takes action* in this verse. God's peace, which doesn't make sense to the world, *does* something. It's active.

It guards. It guards our hearts, and it guards our minds. And it all happens *through Christ Jesus.* How? What does that even mean? Jesus conquered death. That truth is the source of our ultimate peace.

If you watched the television series *This Is Us*, you probably remember Randall and Beth playing "worst-case scenario." They would do this when they found themselves worrying about something. It was usually related to their girls, and it was always amusing. It would start with one of them saying a mild bad thing that *could happen*, and the other one would say something a little bit worse. They would go back and forth this way until they ended at something hilariously horrible and very unlikely to happen. And it always worked because they would end up laughing and realizing that their current situation wasn't all that bad. They could work through it.

You can play worst-case scenario too. With any given scenario, it could end with death and dying and life as we know it coming to a drastic end. But even if that happened, guess what? Jesus conquered death. He already conquered the worst-case scenario.

Our hope and our peace rest securely on the foundation of Jesus Christ. His promises are certain and are not going away. Nothing is more powerful. Nothing is surer. And nothing else gives us the hope and peace our hearts long for when we're navigating the stress and pressure and uncertainty of life.

Here are Jesus's own words. In this passage, he had just explained to his disciples that some hard times were coming: "These things I have spoken to you so that in Me you may have peace. In the world you have tribulation, but take courage; I have overcome the world" (John 16:33 NASB). He taught them the lessons. He modeled what it looks like to love God and love others. And he reminded them that this world offers up some tough stuff. But even so, they could be courageous in the face of it because he'd already overcome the worst-case scenario.

The same is true for us. Amid the stresses and pressures of life, he doesn't promise to swoop in and make everything better. He's more interested in working inside us and equipping us to lean on him during the problems that seem unsolvable. And there, with him, we find peace.

Okay, let's get practical for a moment. You might be thinking, "Sandra, all of this is great. But how do I help my daughter in the real-life, real-time hard stuff? When she's spiraling under the weight of the stress?"

Allie offers some ideas in the corresponding chapter that will set up your daughter to experience the peace of God—the kind that surpasses understanding and transcends the stresses and pressures of her every day. Specifically, Allie talks about three priorities in times of stress—or when trying to keep stress at bay:

Guard your time.
Guard your hope.
Guard your heart.

## Guard Your Time

When you think about your schedule and your family's schedule, is there any breathing room? Are there intentional gaps of time for rest—for doing nothing structured? Do you consistently gather your family around the dinner table for connection and conversation?

A few years ago, I wrote a twenty-eight-day devotional called *Breathing Room*, explaining that breathing room is simply *the space between your current pace and your limits.* We all need space. We need margin. We need rest. It's imperative to stop living at our limits if we want any kind of sustained peace in our lives. To do that, we must come to terms with the fact that *our time is limited, so we must limit what we do with our time.* That means learning to say no. Or learning to say, "Not right now." If our girls can learn the discipline of saying no, it will serve them their entire lives. And it will go a long way toward reducing the load of stress they carry.

If your family is anything like ours, you're the general keeper of the calendar. You're the one who knows who needs to be where, and when. And you're likely the one who can help everyone else bring a bit of balance to their schedule by leading the way.

Remember the prayer of surrender from earlier in this chapter?

That last sentence was "Help me do what I can do and to leave the rest to you." What can *you* do? Consider specific items or activities you might need to unload to reduce stress and pressure. Here are a few ideas for you and your daughter to think about:

- Is there some calendar pruning to do? Some activities you can say no to?
- Do you need to schedule "solitude" as an appointment in the morning or afternoon a few days a week?
- Are there any social media limits you need to set?
- Do any of your relationships need boundaries?
- Is there something you need to change so you can start your day with quiet time, just you and God?

Do your part, then trust him to do his.

## Guard Your Hope

"Guard your hope" sounds a bit odd. But we do often hear the phrase "Don't lose hope." We talk about feeling hopeless, and in the context of stress and pressure, hopelessness is a quick and easy place to land. It's closely connected to feeling alienated or helpless or trapped in circumstances that show no signs of improving. Now that we're adults, our life experiences have taught us that some of the worst situations in which we find ourselves actually *do* improve over time. But our girls haven't lived long enough to know that. It's easy for them to believe that a temporary setback or embarrassment or failure will feel as devastating forever as it does the week it happens. Their peace goes out the window, and hopelessness replaces it because peace and hope are inextricably linked. That's why it's important to speak the truth of hope into your daughter, helping her guard her hope.

I love the word *hope*. It's a good word. We use it in all kinds of contexts, right?

I hope it doesn't rain today.
I hope I get the job.
I hope there's dessert.

That kind of hope is based on what I'm wishing for—my personal desires. But real life happens, and things don't always go my way. My hope is shattered because the event was rained out. Someone else got the job. And, to top it all off, there was no dessert! But that's not real hope. That's personal preference. If my peace is tied to that kind of hope, I will likely lose both.

The hope I'm talking about is different. Real hope—the kind that isn't only about the details of life—points our hearts and minds in a healthy, upward direction. It keeps us going when we're tempted to quit. It gives us patience to trust that all will be worth it. Real hope sits on something solid and sure.

If you are a Christian—a Christ follower—your hope should rest in the promises God has made to you:

- The promise of salvation he made to you and to your daughter the moment you each trusted him as Savior.
- The promise of his presence *with you* regardless of how hard the journey becomes.
- The promise that he will bring good from even the worst things in life.

The writer of Hebrews reminds us that God is ever faithful: "Let us hold unswervingly to the hope we profess, for he who promised is faithful" (10:23). This life can be bumpy and uncomfortable and chaotic at times. Placing our hope in God's promises protects us from discouragement, worry, stress, and the weight of the pressures of life. Our hope is not misplaced when it rests in him. And in that hope, there is peace.

When we don't hold unswervingly to that hope, the stresses and pressures can easily catapult us into the what-if trap. And it's even easier for our girls to fall into it. We start thinking unhealthy thoughts like these:

What if they don't like me?
What if I don't get the promotion?
What if I fail?
What if my kids fail?
What if we don't have enough money?
What if I can't get it all done?
What if I get sick?
What if I lose someone I love?
What if I can't keep up?

Our what-ifs and our girls' what-ifs are not so different. Worry comes naturally, regardless of age. It seems innate to look down the road and anxiously anticipate what's headed our way. Or what *could be* headed our way. Don't get me wrong; it's wise to be prepared. It's good to anticipate and even take refuge at times (Proverbs 27:12). But when the stresses and pressures of life cause us to turn to worry rather than to our heavenly Father, we quickly lose hope. We become anxious.

So how do we guard our hope? And how do we help our girls guard theirs? Again, through prayer and petition. Our Philippians passage tells us, "In every situation, by prayer and petition, with thanksgiving, present your requests to God" (4:6). That's the place and the posture where we are able to lean on him for guidance and direction and instruction. It's the place where we lay down our stresses and fears and allow him to handle the part that isn't ours to handle. And he's so faithful to meet us there. More than that, he meets us there with an incredible hope. And following quick on the heels of that hope is an amazing peace.

## Guard Your Heart

"Above all else, guard your heart, for everything you do flows from it" (Proverbs 4:23). I love this verse. Other versions say, ". . . from it flow the springs of life."

When our kids were little, Andy and I got in the habit of asking a series of "heart checkup" questions as we put them to bed. It started right after prayer time one night with Andy simply asking Andrew, our oldest, "Andrew, is everything okay in your heart?"

Andrew smiled and said, "Yes, sir, Daddy." And that began a routine with all three of our kids. In his wisdom, Andy decided the first step to guarding their hearts was to help them get in the habit of paying attention to what was going on in there. Over time we added several other questions. Eventually the list looked like this:

- Is everything okay in your heart?
- Did anybody hurt your feelings today?
- Are you mad at anybody?
- Are you worried about anything?
- Did anybody break a promise to you today?
- Is there anything you want to tell me but you're not sure how?

This was our routine for years. The questions became so engrained that one night as Andy was putting a tired Allie to bed, she lay down, closed her eyes, and said, "Daddy, everything is okay

93

in my heart. Nobody hurt my feelings. I'm not mad at anybody. I'm not worried. And nobody broke a promise. Good night."

Cute story, I know. But really, when it comes to equipping and motivating our girls to examine and guard their hearts, it's pretty much us or nobody. And the author of that statement from Proverbs is not wrong. The condition of our children's hearts is *above all else* because their emotional health determines their relational health. Our relationship with them and their relationship with their heavenly Father are of utmost importance. When tough stuff comes, when the stresses and pressures our girls face close in, it's all about doing what we can do and then coming to him with our prayers and petitions, laying everything before him with thanksgiving. "And the peace of God, which transcends all understanding, will guard your hearts and your minds in Christ Jesus" (Philippians 4:7).

How's your heart? How's your daughter's heart? Get in the habit of finding out.

I'll wrap up this chapter with one of the most memorized passages in all of Scripture. We talked about it in chapter 6 too:

> **The** LORD is my shepherd, I lack nothing.
>     He makes me lie down in green pastures,
> he leads me beside quiet waters,
>     he refreshes my soul. **(PSALM 23:1–3)**

Isn't that amazing? I love that he *refreshes* my soul. Other translations, such as the NASB, say he "restores" my soul. The Hebrew word translated here means "return" or "turn back." As the worries and stresses and busyness drain our souls, our good heavenly Father knows we need refreshing, restoring, a returning to peacefulness. He brings about all of that when we allow him to shepherd us—to lead us, guide us, provide for us.

So let's get in the habit of crying out to God in our times of need. Let's fall to our knees and make our requests known. And then trust him to do what only he can do. We'll be changed. Our girls will be changed. We'll have the deep breath we need in the chaos of life.

And the peace of God, which transcends all understanding, will guard our hearts and our minds in Christ Jesus, because he has overcome the world!

# CHAPTER 8

# Writing a Good Story

Do you have a story about when you went "all in" with God? A pivotal moment when it suddenly hit you that you didn't want to be half-hearted anymore? You knew you needed to get off the fence and follow in the ways of Jesus in *all* the areas of your life?

You certainly don't have to have one of those moments to be a Christian. But I did have one, and I remember it well. It was the fall of my junior year of college. I was walking back to my dorm room on the Georgia Tech campus after an evening Bible study I regularly attended. The woman teaching us had just started a study on the book of Philippians. That particular evening, she had read from chapter 1 and talked about Paul's letter to the Christians in the city of Philippi—thus the name of the book, Philippians. Paul was telling them how thankful he was for the way they were growing in their faith and helping him reach new people for Jesus. He continued the thought with this: ". . . being confident of this, that he who began a good work in you will carry it on to completion until the day of Christ Jesus" (Philippians 1:6).

Something about the word *completion* sent me reeling. I couldn't stop wondering if maybe I had placed some roadblocks in the way of God working toward my completion, or at least my progress. An honest look showed me one of the roadblocks I had been ignoring. It was a relationship. It was a dating relationship I was hanging on to even though I knew it was time to let it go. The guy was kind and thoughtful and smart. He was even a churchgoing guy, though I always wondered if that was more for me than for himself. Even so, something in me knew he wasn't God's choice for me. But I was hanging on to the relationship anyway.

So that night, walking past the stadium on Bobby Dodd Way to my dorm, I stopped. I looked up at the sky and, like a weirdo, started talking out loud. I said something along the lines of, "God, I know there is no true joy and fulfillment outside your will for my life. I'm just going to let you have *all* the categories. I'll probably do a little tug-of-war here and there with you, but ultimately, I want your will for my life."

I know it doesn't sound like much. But for me it *was* much. It was pivotal for me, not because of that one relationship decision but because it set the tone for future decision-making. It placed me on a different path—a path of submitting to God. I chose a mindset that basically said this: When what *I want* conflicts with what *God wants* for me, I will go with what *God wants* every single time.

I found a freedom that night. And looking back, I have no regrets. In fact, about six months later I met a cute guy who filled in for my regular Bible study teacher. Thirty-six years later, he's sitting beside me while I type these words.

And it boiled down to *a decision*. A decision to submit to God. A decision I'll never regret.

Speaking of decisions, here's a fun fact: Did you know that on any given day, you make somewhere around thirty-five thousand conscious decisions?[10] From the time your eyes open in the morning to the time they close at night, you make approximately thirty-five thousand decisions. Not all of them are big, bold, high-pressure decisions like choosing the right doctor to do your surgery or assessing the viability of a new career path. Some of them are little ones, like which shoes to wear or whether to toss an umbrella into your bag on the way out the door in the morning.

Think of how many times you look at your phone and make a decision: To answer or not? *Nope, I don't recognize that number. Definitely not answering.* When to respond to a text? *Urgent? Nope, it can wait.* Do I use an exclamation point or not? *I don't want to come across as too eager, so maybe no exclamation point. But I don't want to sound boring, so maybe I should use it?* I tend to overthink exclamation-point use because Allie once informed me that when I text her and put a period at the end of the sentence, she thinks I'm mad at her. "Mom, either use an exclamation point so I'll know you're happy, or no punctuation at all so I won't think you're mad." Oh, okay. Here's the thing though: I had Mrs. Kisalus and Mrs. Green for English teachers when I was at Dublin High School. They ingrained in me the importance of proper punctuation, and to this day I can't get away from it. So there's about a 99 percent chance I'm not mad when I punctuate.

Anyway, back to decisions—thirty-five thousand of 'em. That's a lot of decisions throughout your day! (I just spent four and a half minutes wrestling with whether to use exclamation points in the previous sentences. I went back and forth. Took two out, and left one in. It felt right.)

Sometimes our decisions are simple right-versus-wrong kinds of decisions. Like, should I roll through this four-way stop since no other cars are coming? Or should I send a quick one-word text even though I'm driving? In those cases, there is a right answer and a wrong one. So the decision should be fairly easy to make.

Some decisions are bigger and even more obvious than that, but we might struggle with them. Will I make the moral or the immoral choice? Will I make the honest or the dishonest decision? You probably have a relatively easy time with these because, first of all, they're obvious. And second, most of us have lived long enough to know that the consequences of bad choices have the potential to rock our worlds. And we don't love that, right?

But some decisions are harder to sort through. Maybe because we have a preference but also an inkling that our preference is the wrong decision. Or because other people are encouraging us in a direction, but we're not sure their motives are right. Or because occasionally there's more than one good choice and we just don't know which way to go.

I want to suggest two questions to whip out when you're faced with hard decisions. And these are great questions for your daughter too. Have them handy when she faces tricky options in her decision-making.

## 1. What Story Do I Want to Tell?

Life is complicated. A lot of circumstances, and details, and actions of others impact our personal stories and are outside our control. But the majority of our life stories are most influenced by the decisions we make.

I am writing the story of my life one decision at a time. So are you. And so is your daughter. When a decision looms in front of us, we typically think of it in the short term: How does this affect me today? What do I prefer right now? But what if we pivot from that way of thinking to this: When all is said and done and this situation is in the rearview mirror, what story do I want to tell? What will I want to say about the decision I'm about to make?

What story do you want to tell in your next job interview? To a new boss or coworker? What story do you want to tell your daughter when she's a little older and faces her own career choices or relationship choices or friendship issues?

As you coach your precious girl, help her ask it this way: "What story do I want to tell *my* future daughter someday?" "What story do I want to tell my future husband?" "What story will deliver the least amount of regret when I think it over later?"

With friendship decisions, clothing choices, entertainment options, and middle school drama, Allie and I often phrased it like this: "What would be lovely?" or "What is the lovelier option?"

Take a look at these real-life adult examples. Maybe you can relate.

### EXAMPLES

Your boss presented an opportunity that would provide a decent bonus at the end of the year but would take advantage of a client. You said yes even though you didn't feel good about it. A nice paycheck came, but every time you see that client, or think back to that situation, or carry the purse you bought with the bonus, you have regret because you participated.

*The better story*: Your boss presented a shady opportunity, and you said, "No thanks," and lost your job. But sleep comes easily at night.

———

Your friend asked you to lie for her. You hate lying, but you did it because you didn't want to disappoint her. The truth came out, and a group of people no longer trust what you say.

*The better story*: Your friend asked you to lie for her. You looked her in the eye and assured her of your care for her but let her know you're not a liar. She got mad, but she eventually got over it and she never doubts that you're a trustworthy person.

As Andy says in *Better Decisions, Fewer Regrets*, "The decisions you're in the middle of making right now . . . this week . . . today . . . are going to be reduced to a story you tell. Once it's behind you, it's a story. Period."[11] We all desire to have a story that makes us proud, not embarrassed. We hope to sit down with our kids and our grandkids and tell our stories without having to skip major sections.

The apostle Paul is the quintessential example of someone who made hard decisions because he knew the story he wanted to be able to tell: Faithfulness to his God. Moral authority to influence others. A story that would inspire. And at the end of our Philippians passage, he says to the people of Philippi and to us, "Whatever you have learned or received or heard from me, or seen in me—put it into practice. And the God of peace will be with you" (4:9).

Paul said this because the Philippian people didn't have their own copies of the Scriptures. They couldn't read the Bible and emulate the ways of Jesus. To be Jesus followers, they relied on verbal instructions. They needed someone who had encountered Jesus personally and who modeled what it looked like to follow him. So Paul said, "Watch me, listen to me, and emulate me as I emulate Christ."

When we make decisions that honor God, we have peace. When we allow the ways of Jesus to influence our decision-making, we have collections of stories we can tell to inspire others. We can take a deep breath and know our hearts are at peace. We can lay our heads on our pillows at night and experience the peace God promises.

There is a second question we can ask when faced with tough decisions. This simple question removes from the table many lesser options and brings clarity out of the fog.

## 2. What Is the Wise Thing to Do?

Let's pause a second and talk about regret. Regret is like a weight. After we make a poor decision, regret is the emotion related to the consequences of that poor choice. It hangs around our neck like a literal weight sometimes. It pays to stop and consider the encumbrance and investigate how we wound up in this regretful place with painful consequences for ourselves, and possibly for the people most important to us. On closer examination we may find that our poor decisions, the ones that brought about significant consequences, were often preceded by a *series* of unwise decisions.

> "There's nothing *wrong* with going to lunch with him. Everybody has to eat lunch." (And we're right.)
>
> → "There's nothing *wrong* with working late, even though he's working late too." (And we're right.)
>
> → "There's nothing *wrong* with having a few drinks after work. Good grief, everybody needs to unwind." (And we're right-ish.)
>
> → "There's nothing *wrong* with riding together. Saving gas is good!" (Okay, sure.)

You can see how the gap incrementally closes and how we baby-step right up to the line between *not exactly wrong* and *absolutely wrong*. By that point, we're so close that stepping over it takes shockingly little effort.

If we had stopped at the very first decision and asked, "What is the *wise* thing to do?" and answered it honestly, we wouldn't have made it past lunch. We wouldn't be facing broken relationships and possibly a fractured family. We wouldn't be holding the weight of regret that followed an unwise decision.

I realize that's an extreme example, but I really, really want to get your attention. Often the consequences of unwise decision-making *are* extreme—for ourselves and for our girls. The beauty of the wisdom question is that it backs us away from that sometimes-magnetic line: *How close can I get to doing wrong without actually doing wrong?* The wisdom question says, "Hey! Hey! Step back from the line! Your toes are dangling over the edge, and it won't take much to push you over to the place where regret lives."

Think back to your biggest regret. The one you *really* wish you could go back and undo. The one you have trouble erasing from your memory because it seems to haunt you. And maybe it taunts you and lies to you about your worth. What if you'd had "What is the wise thing to do?" in your decision-making arsenal way back then? Think you would've made a different decision?

Let's equip our girls on *this side* of those temptations with some tools in their toolboxes for harnessing wisdom in their decision-making.

One of my favorite things about the book of Proverbs is that Solomon, a super-wise guy by all historical accounts, personified wisdom in his writings. He gave wisdom a personality and a voice. I like it because it feels like someone I want to be friends with. Maybe someone I'd want as a mentor. But also, I'd be a little scared of her.

Look at Proverbs 8:1–21:

> **Does** not wisdom call out?
>> Does not understanding raise her voice?
> At the highest point along the way,
>> where the paths meet, she takes her stand;
> beside the gate leading into the city,
>> at the entrance, she cries aloud:
> "To you, O people, I call out;
>> I raise my voice to all mankind.
> You who are simple, gain prudence;
>> you who are foolish, set your hearts on it.
> Listen, for I have trustworthy things to say;
>> I open my lips to speak what is right.
> My mouth speaks what is true,

for my lips detest wickedness.
All the words of my mouth are just;
    none of them is crooked or perverse.
To the discerning all of them are right;
    they are upright to those who have found
        knowledge.
Choose my instruction instead of silver,
    knowledge rather than choice gold,
for wisdom is more precious than rubies,
    and nothing you desire can compare with her.


"I, wisdom, dwell together with prudence;
    I possess knowledge and discretion.
To fear the LORD is to hate evil;
    I hate pride and arrogance,
      evil behavior and perverse speech.
Counsel and sound judgment are mine;
    I have insight, I have power.
By me kings reign
    and rulers issue decrees that are just;
by me princes govern,
    and nobles—all who rule on earth.
I love those who love me,
    and those who seek me find me.
With me are riches and honor,
    enduring wealth and prosperity.
My fruit is better than fine gold;
    what I yield surpasses choice silver.
I walk in the way of righteousness,
    along the paths of justice,
bestowing a rich inheritance on those who love me
    and making their treasuries full."

Isn't that amazing? Wouldn't you want to have a friend like that walking around with you, giving you advice and always ready for a consultation? Get this: you do. Wisdom is one of the attributes of God that is available to us through the Holy Spirit, who lives in us. And he delights in illuminating our way, even in our mundane day-to-day decision-making. He probably won't speak audibly, but he may give you clarity through Scripture during your quiet time. Or he'll speak to you through a wise counselor or friend. Or he'll simply bring clarity out of the chaos of your thoughts. He'll whisper wisdom to you when you have yourself in a position to hear. And often, in simply asking for wisdom, you're positioned to hear.

I took a passage out of the book of Colossians and turned it into a prayer for my kids. In these verses, Paul expresses to the people in Colossae how he's been praying for them. Part of his prayer is specifically for them to have wisdom. As they navigated life as Jesus followers in a world that thought Jesus-following was crazy, he knew they'd need loads of wisdom and knowledge and understanding:

> **For** this reason, since the day we heard about you, we have not stopped praying for you. We continually ask God to fill you with the knowledge of his will through all the wisdom and understanding that the Spirit gives, so that you may live a life worthy of the Lord and please him in every way: bearing fruit in every good work, growing in the knowledge of God, being strengthened with all power according to his glorious might so that you may have great endurance and patience, and giving joyful thanks to the Father, who has qualified you to share in the inheritance of his holy people in the kingdom of light.
>
> **(COLOSSIANS 1:9–12)**

Here's the way I pray it for Allie and others I love:

*Heavenly Father, please fill Allie with the knowledge of your will in all spiritual wisdom and understanding so that she will walk in a manner worthy of you and please you in all her ways. Let her bear fruit as she serves you, and let her knowledge of you and her relationship with you always increase. Give her your strength and your power to overcome temptation and to live patiently and joyfully. Thank you for the promise of your presence within her. In Jesus's name. Amen.*

In the years I've prayed this prayer for Allie, I've been gifted glimpse after glimpse of God's answers to those requests. Those glimpses fill my heart with an unspeakable joy.

As we wrap up this chapter, I'd like to say one more thing to you, mom. It's never too late to start writing a different story. If you have a track record of poor decision-making and you carry the weight of regret around with you, you *can* be free from that. Your heavenly Father has strong shoulders and would love for you to hand it over. While you can't go back and rewrite chapters of your story, you can allow God to reframe them, redeem them, and use them for his glory and your good—and maybe even the good of your daughter at the appropriate time. So start today, asking the two questions and seeking God's guidance in the midst of *your* decision-making.

What story do you want to tell from here? And what's the wise thing to do? You are *not* alone.

# Final Thoughts
# for Moms

You did it, mama. You made it through the chapters and discussions and activities. Hopefully you had a great time with your girl along the way. I feel like we've been on a little journey together, and it's hard to say goodbye!

Allie and I have prayed for you. We prayed for you as we wrote this book. And we continue to pray that God will take the time you each invested and bring about an extraordinary return. We also hope this content and these past eight interactions will help you to have ongoing rich and meaningful conversations in the days and years ahead.

One of the goals of this book, as we expressed in the introduction, was for you to guide your daughter in her faith journey, helping her form a personal faith that impacts everything she does. One that informs her decision-making, gives her confidence that God loves her and has amazing plans for her life, and assures her of his presence even on the hardest days.

As a backdrop to all the topics, we focused on Philippians 4:4–9:

**Rejoice** in the Lord always. I will say it again: Rejoice! Let your gentleness be evident to all. The Lord is near. Do not be anxious about anything, but in every situation, by prayer and petition, with thanksgiving, present your requests to God. And the peace of God, which transcends all understanding, will guard your hearts and your minds in Christ Jesus.

Finally, brothers and sisters, whatever is true, whatever is noble, whatever is right, whatever is pure, whatever is lovely, whatever is admirable—if anything is excellent or praiseworthy—think about such things. Whatever you have learned or received or heard from me, or seen in me—put it into practice. And the God of peace will be with you.

So as you navigate this beautiful—and sometimes messy—journey of being mom to your amazing daughter, keep a few things at the forefront of your mind.

1. The things that happen in the heart are oh so important. So keep a check on yours and hers. And remind her to do the same. Solomon's words are great for regular mind renewal: "Above all else, guard your heart, for everything you do flows from it" (Proverbs 4:23).

2. Encourage your daughter to develop and maintain the habit of spending time alone with God. I always suggest to moms that they model it, encourage it, and make it easy. Let her see you prioritizing this habit. Encourage her to find a sweet spot of time and space of her own. And make it easy by ensuring she has an age-appropriate Bible, maybe a great devotional, a fun journal—things that will set her up for success in this area.

3. Pray for her, and with her, as you have opportunity, especially

when she presents a tough situation or set of circumstances she's facing. Developing a habit of turning to our heavenly Father with all our difficulties and challenges is such a win. After all, he made your daughter. He loves her. And he created her *with* purpose and *for* a purpose.

I'm convinced that as you encourage your daughter toward an enduring, real-world faith of her own that frames the other variables of her life, she will find purpose and peace regardless of what comes her way. And the cherry on top? You'll always have a role to play in her journey.

Love,

## Sandra

# MEET ME
## IN THE
# MIDDLE

# Introduction to
# MEET ME IN THE MIDDLE
# Discussions

Welcome to the section where the two of you get to put the chapters into practice and have some fun along the way!

*This* is the biggest reason we wanted to write this book. Though certainly not perfect, our relationship with each other has been so important for both of us in every season of life so far. And we really want that for the two of you!

We hope these activities and discussions will deepen your faith, of course. But we also hope they will deepen your relationship. This is a time to share what's on your hearts. As you truly listen to each other, we believe you will cultivate a richer and closer relationship.

Here are a couple of things to remember:

- Get ready by taking a look at this section before your time together. Read the questions and be thinking about your responses.

- Plan for any activities that require a bit of prep. That will help you make the most of your time together.

This is not meant to be a teaching time or a one-sided conversation. You both have so much to learn about each other and from each other. Your gifts and talents and personalities are probably varied and different. So leverage those differences and learn. Understanding each other better will serve you well now *and* in the seasons to come.

For a mother-daughter duo who are vastly different from each other (Allie is more creative and carefree, while Sandra is more structured and analytical), some of our richest times have been when we've leaned in the other person's direction and tried to understand things from their perspective rather than from our own. We hope the same for you.

Okay, ladies, you've got this. Lean in, be honest, and enjoy this time together.

# Foundations Matter

### What Are You Good At?

- If you could snap your fingers and be immediately excellent at one thing, what would it be? It could be something reasonable or completely unreasonable. But you have to explain why you picked it!

- What is something you're good at now but were not always good at? Take turns sharing. Any funny stories about it?

### The Fruit of the Spirit

- Read Galatians 5:22–23 together: "The fruit of the Spirit is love, joy, peace, forbearance [patience], kindness, goodness, faithfulness, gentleness and self-control."

- Which fruit of the Spirit do you think you need more of in your life? Moms, underline in one color pen or pencil, and girls underline in another color. Compare notes! Talk together about what it would look like to have more of the one fruit you need most. Remember, the Helper (the Holy Spirit) is *with you*. Ask him to help you demonstrate more of these fruits in the moments when you're running low.

> I have a *heavenly Father* who loves me, a *Savior* who gave his life for me, and a *Helper* who is in it with me.

- Celebrate each other when you see those fruits of the Spirit demonstrated in each other!

117

## Quiet Time

- Are you set up to have regular time alone with God? Take turns answering the following questions out loud, and discuss any actions you each need to take:
  - ☐ Would morning, midday, or evening work best for me to be consistent in my time with God?
  - ☐ Do I have a cozy spot I can designate as the place where I read my Bible and pray?
  - ☐ Do I have a Bible of my own that is easy to read and study?
  - ☐ What other tools do I need to have handy? (A special mug for a warm drink, a journal for notes, pens, colored pencils, highlighters, a commentary or devotional book, etc.)
- Looking for an outing? Anybody like to shop? Pick a store that has cute mugs, and choose a quiet-time mug for each other. Make sure to pick one you think the other person would like, not necessarily one *you* like!

Here's our main verse for the whole book. Put it where you will see it often. Make it a part of your routine to read it every day. Maybe even start memorizing it!

Rejoice in the Lord always. I will say it again: Rejoice!
Let your gentleness be evident to all. The Lord is near.
Do not be anxious about anything, but in every situation, by
prayer and petition, with thanksgiving, present your requests to
God. And the peace of God, which transcends all understanding,
will guard your hearts and your minds in Christ Jesus.

Finally, brothers and sisters, whatever is true, whatever is noble,
whatever is right, whatever is pure, whatever is lovely, whatever
is admirable—if anything is excellent or praiseworthy—
think about such things. Whatever you have learned
or received or heard from me, or seen in
me—put it into practice. And the God
of peace will be with you.

**—PHILIPPIANS 4:4–9**

# You Are Who *God* Says You Are

*What is one thing you don't like that you feel you should like?*

*Have you ever pretended to like something you didn't actually like? Why did you pretend to like it? Was it to get a specific person's attention? Was it so people would admire or like you more?*

Grab those pens again, and each of you fill in a blank. If you can't think of anything current, think of something from earlier in your life.

(Daughter) I am not _____ enough.

(Mom) I am not _____ enough.

Talk to each other about what it is like to feel less than. Also discuss what it would look like to dwell on what

> See what great love the Father has lavished on us, that we should be called children of God! And that is what we are! **(1 JOHN 3:1)**

God says is true about you. (You are made in his image. You don't have to change or pretend or lose hope.)

Read the following verses to remind yourselves of who you are in Christ. Maybe pick one of them, turn it into a prayer, and pray it for each other.

**See** what great love the Father has lavished on us, that we should be called children of God! And that is what we are! (1 JOHN 3:1)

> **I** praise you because I am fearfully and
> wonderfully made;
> your works are wonderful,
> I know that full well. (PSALM 139:14)

**You** are a chosen people, a royal priesthood, a holy nation, God's special possession, that you may declare the praises of him who called you out of darkness into his wonderful light. (1 PETER 2:9)

**Because** of his great love for us, God, who is rich in mercy, made us alive in Christ even when we were dead in our transgressions—it is by grace you have been saved. (EPHESIANS 2:4–5)

**Finally,** brothers and sisters, whatever is true, whatever is noble, whatever is right, whatever is pure, whatever is lovely, whatever is admirable—if anything is excellent or praiseworthy—think about such things. (PHILIPPIANS 4:8)

# No Win in Comparison

Share a memory of comparing yourself to someone else and the feelings that resulted. Can you think of a time when you felt "less than" and another time when you felt you came out on top? Did feeling this way help or hurt your relationship with that person?

> Celebrate what God has given others, and leverage what God has given you.

Honestly share with each other three or four areas where you tend to compare yourself with other people. Respond to each one with, "Mom, you are God's handiwork, and he has a plan just for you. So fix your eyes on Jesus." Or "[Daughter's name], you are God's handiwork, and he has a plan just for you. So fix your eyes on Jesus."

Okay, here's an amazing, heart-strengthening activity to do together. Pick a person whose successes make you feel less than, maybe someone who received or achieved something you were hoping for. Write a note of congratulations, or simply express that you're happy for him or her. Mail or deliver it. If you're up for adding some baked goods to the delivery, try the following recipe. It's one of our favorites!

**COMPARISON SAYS:** Fix your eyes on the people around you.
**CULTURE SAYS:** Fix your eyes on yourself.
**GOD SAYS:** Fix your eyes on Jesus.

# Allie and Sandra's Snickerdoodles

**YIELD:** 3 dozen

## INGREDIENTS

2½ cups flour (we like to use half all-purpose and half whole wheat)

2 teaspoons cream of tartar

1 teaspoon baking soda

½ teaspoon salt

1 cup (2 sticks) butter, melted

½ cup light brown sugar

1 cup sugar

1½ teaspoons vanilla extract

½ teaspoon almond extract (if you don't have any, just use more vanilla)

2 eggs, room temperature

1 tablespoon ground cinnamon

3 tablespoons sugar

## DIRECTIONS

1. Preheat oven to 400° F.
2. Using a whisk, combine flour, cream of tartar, baking soda, and salt. Set aside.
3. Using a mixer, mix together melted butter and both sugars.
4. Blend in vanilla and almond extracts.
5. Add eggs and mix for 2 to 3 minutes.
6. Reduce mixer speed and slowly add flour mixture until well combined.
7. Some people say to let the batter rest for 15 to 20 minutes. Sometimes we do; sometimes we don't.
8. Combine cinnamon and sugar in a shallow dish. Scoop dough and form into 1½ inch balls. Roll balls in cinnamon-sugar mixture until coated.
9. Place on parchment-lined cookie sheet with room to spread (2 to 3 inches apart). Don't flatten them; let the hot oven do that work for you.
10. Bake for 7 to 9 minutes or until cookies are lightly browned. They should be firm but with puffy, soft centers.

# Family Is Forever

This week, have your *Meet Me in the Middle* conversation at your favorite local coffee shop. Afterward, head to a card shop together to choose a special card for someone in your family you need to appreciate.

*When was the last imaginary conversation you had? You know, the one where you have a back-and-forth conversation in your head, you say everything perfectly, and your words are so stellar the other person has no comeback?*

*Who was it with? Why did you have it?*

Let your gentleness be evident to all. **(PHILIPPIANS 4:5)**

Three great things you can choose to exhibit toward your family are *appreciation*, *forgiveness*, and *gentleness*. Rank them in order, starting with the one that comes easiest for you.

| **(Mom)** | **(Daughter)** |
|---|---|
| 1. _____ | 1. _____ |
| 2. _____ | 2. _____ |
| 3. _____ | 3. _____ |

*Is there someone in your family you need to forgive? It can be for something big or something small. Discuss together how you can follow the four Rs (Recognize, Release, Remember, Restore) and forgive that person.*

*When it comes to your family, "let your gentleness be evident to all" (Philippians 4:5). Which one person in your family do you most need to be gentler with? How can you remind yourself, and each other, to be gentler in the following days?*

Pick someone in your family (other than your mom/daughter) to whom you want to write a note of appreciation. Head to a card shop together!

Whatever is true, whatever is noble, whatever is right, whatever is pure, whatever is lovely, whatever is admirable—if anything is excellent or praiseworthy— think about such things. **(PHILIPPIANS 4:8)**

# Finding Your People

Read 1 Corinthians 13:4–8:

> **Love** is patient, love is kind. It does not envy, it does not boast, it is not proud. It does not dishonor others, it is not self-seeking, it is not easily angered, it keeps no record of wrongs. Love does not delight in evil but rejoices with the truth. It always protects, always trusts, always hopes, always perseveres.
>
> Love never fails.

Pick two characteristics that you think best describe the other person: patient, kind, secure, unpretentious, humble, honoring, selfless, slow to anger, forgiving, truthful, protective of others, trusting, hopeful, strong.

My mom is great at loving by being _____ and _____.

My daughter is great at loving by being _____ and _____.

Which two do you think you most need to work on?

(Daughter) I need to love better by being
more _____ and _____.

(Mom) I need to love better by being
more _____ and _____.

*"Be the person the person you're looking for is looking for."* Go back and forth saying traits that you want to have in a friend/boyfriend/spouse/future spouse. Write them below.

_____
_____
_____
_____
_____
_____

*Do you demonstrate those traits in your life? If not, or if you need to improve a bit, how can you take steps in that direction?*

_____
_____
_____
_____
_____

Together, read Allie's Rules for High School. As you read, comment about what you think of each one. Daughters, hang a copy in your room or on your bathroom mirror where you can see it often and be reminded!

# Allie's Rules for High School

1. Surround yourself with people who build you up, not people who tear you down.

2. Treat your kisses like you have a limited supply.

3. Guard your heart. Seriously . . . your heart is precious.

4. Stay vertical. Set your physical boundaries and stick to them.

5. Have an accountability partner and be willing to tell HER everything.

6. Be so so so so so so so SO SO SO SO careful who you date.

7. If you're wondering if you should break up with him, break up with him.

8. If your girl gets broken up with, go buy her a stuffed animal, a blanket, candy, and lots and lots of ice cream. (Other gifts are acceptable too.)

9. Pray, PRAY, PRAY! Don't ever forget how much you need God.

10. Have a quiet time. It may seem like a hassle, but it will help you stay close to God.

11. Be nice to your parents. They love you and want the best for you, so if you disagree with them, just realize that they are a lot smarter than you . . . sorry about it.

12. If you find yourself lying to your parents or other adults in your life, backtrack and get out of that situation IMMEDIATELY. You are somewhere you do not want to be.

13. Never be afraid to say no. It's better to be a wimp than dead.

14. When you fall on your face, get back up and keep moving (literally and figuratively).

15. Journal so you can look back and see what God has done in your life.

16. Even when you don't want to, GO TO CHURCH!

17. If it's not classy, don't do it.

18. Don't judge. Even when people are doing things you don't agree with, show them love.

19. Pause before you speak . . . this will prevent a lot of problems.

20. Selfies are for faces.

# Fear Is *Not* in Charge

We talked in this chapter about fears. Our Philippians passage tells us that the Lord is near. God's nearness is a powerful thing when we're afraid. And there's power in mom/daughter nearness too. Or even in mentor nearness!

> My God will meet all your needs according to the riches of his glory in Christ Jesus. **(PHILIPPIANS 4:19)**

Today, find a nearby park, neighborhood, or trail and take a walk together. While you're walking, talk through some of the following questions. (If it's raining where you are today, maybe have an ice cream sundae instead? That's probably what we would do.)

- What is something silly you are afraid of?
- What is something serious you are afraid of?
- Can you think of a decision you made based on fear that you wish you had made differently? (Here are some examples: You received an invitation to do something you've never done before, but you said no because you were afraid you'd fail or not be good at it. Or you hung out with someone you shouldn't have because you were afraid of saying no, and then you were pressured to do something you wish you hadn't.)
- Is anyone in your life—maybe a friend, coworker, or family member—making decisions based on fear that are negatively affecting the people around them?

The three truths we talked about that help fight our fear are these:

God loves you.
God provides for you.
God has a plan for you.

Rank them in order from easiest to hardest to remember when fear comes knocking at your door!

*In Allie's chapter, she encouraged girls who struggle with clinical mental health disorders to open up to a safe person. Take a moment to talk about the prevalence of mental health problems and how they have affected you or someone you know. If applicable, what steps do either of you need to take to get help?*

The Lord is near. **(PHILIPPIANS 4:5)**

# Peace in the Chaos

Spa day!

Nothing says "stress management" like a trip to a salon or spa. So today, have your discussion while getting a pedicure. Or make this quick and easy homemade facial and enjoy an at-home spa treatment together. Or do both!

## Oatmeal Facial Mask for Two

### DIRECTIONS

1. Wash your face with soap and water.
2. Combine the following ingredients in a medium-sized bowl:
   - 1 cup hot water
   - 2/3 cup oatmeal
3. Let sit for 3 minutes.
4. Add to oatmeal:
   - 4 tablespoons plain yogurt
   - 4 tablespoons honey
   - 1 egg white
5. Stir together well.
6. Spread a thick layer of the mask onto your face and leave on for 10 to 15 minutes.
7. Rinse well with warm water and then use your favorite moisturizer for a soft finish.
8. While your faces are beautifying under the mask, go ahead and have your discussion for this chapter. Unless that's stressful. If so, wait until after you've enjoyed your facial.

Share with each other three things you are currently stressing about. Try to be specific. Share more than three if you need to. After your facial, find a quiet spot to bring your requests to God and pray together. Use the Philippians passage as a guide: "Do not be anxious about anything, but in every situation, by prayer and petition, with thanksgiving, present your requests to God" (Philippians 4:6).

*Heavenly Father, I'm feeling pretty stressed right now about _____. I do see something I can be thankful for about this though. Thank you for _____. Would you show me what I need to do and then give me the ability to leave the rest to you?*

As it relates to each of your schedules, do you need some breathing room? If so, answer the following questions to help you figure out how to create that space.

- Is there some calendar pruning to do? Some activities you can say no to?
- Do you need to schedule "solitude" as an appointment in the morning or afternoon a few days a week?
- Are there any social media limits you need to set?
- Do any of your relationships need boundaries?
- Is there something you need to change so you can start your day with quiet time, just you and God?

Do not be anxious about anything, but in every situation, by prayer and petition, with thanksgiving, present your requests to God. And the peace of God, which transcends all understanding, will guard your hearts and your minds in Christ Jesus. **(PHILIPPIANS 4:6–7)**

# Writing a Good Story

Mom, share with your girl a decision you're glad you made and a decision where you wish you had made a different choice.

### Decision-Making Questions

1. What story do I want to tell?     2. What is the wise thing to do?

*For the decision you wish you had made differently, how could one (or both) of the decision-making questions have helped you make a better decision?*

*What is a decision you are currently making? Examples: Maybe it's deciding whether to take a job opportunity (for mom) or deciding your plans for the weekend (for daughter). How can you use the two decision-making questions to help make the best decision?*

Girls, remember in your chapter when you took a look at the following questions? Now talk through them with your mom. Hey, moms, why don't you take a stab at it too?

*What do you want your life to look like twenty years from now (job, location, hobbies, goals, etc.)?*

_____

_____

_____

Whatever you have learned or received or heard from me, or seen in me—put it into practice. And the God of peace will be with you. **(PHILIPPIANS 4:9)**

*What people do you want to have in your life twenty years from now?*

_____

_____

*What words do you want people to use when they describe you twenty years from now?*

_____

_____

_____

*What do you want to have accomplished twenty years from now?*

_____

_____

_____

We continually ask God to fill you with the knowledge of his will through all the wisdom and understanding that the Spirit gives, so that you may live a life worthy of the Lord and please him in every way. **(COLOSSIANS 1:9–10)**

*Who do you want to be twenty years from now?*

_____

_____

_____

Here's a prayer I (Sandra) have prayed regularly for Allie, and for my boys, since they were little. I took it from Colossians 1:9–12. Allie and I can't think of a better way to wrap up this *Meet Me in the Middle* journey together than for you to pray this prayer for each other.

> If any of you lacks wisdom, you should ask God, who gives generously to all without finding fault, and it will be given to you. **(JAMES 1:5)**

*Heavenly Father, please fill _____ with the knowledge of your will in all spiritual wisdom and understanding so that she will walk in a manner worthy of you and please you in all her ways. Let her bear fruit as she serves you, and let her knowledge of you and her relationship with you always increase. Give her your strength and your power to overcome temptation and to live patiently and joyfully. Thank you for the promise of your presence within her. In Jesus's name. Amen.*

We hope this time of reading your chapters and discussing these important topics has been helpful for you. We also pray that your relationship now is deeper and richer than when you started the journey. Know that we both have prayed that your mom-daughter relationship gets better and better with each passing year. And we've prayed that your faith in your heavenly Father impacts your everyday lives, for the rest of your lives!

## Sandra and Allie

# FOR
# DAUGHTERS

Rejoice in the Lord always. I will say it again: Rejoice!
Let your gentleness be evident to all. The Lord is near.
Do not be anxious about anything, but in every situation, by
prayer and petition, with thanksgiving, present your requests to
God. And the peace of God, which transcends all understanding,
will guard your hearts and your minds in Christ Jesus.

Finally, brothers and sisters, whatever is true, whatever is noble,
whatever is right, whatever is pure, whatever is lovely, whatever
is admirable—if anything is excellent or praiseworthy—
think about such things. Whatever you have learned
or received or heard from me, or seen in
me—put it into practice. And the God
of peace will be with you.

**—PHILIPPIANS 4:4–9**

# Introduction for Daughters

Hey, friends!

My name is Allie, and I'm so excited you're here. I'm glad you're coming on this journey with my mom and me. Let me tell you why.

I know life can be stressful, frustrating, confusing, and sometimes downright hard. Let me just say, I don't know everything (obviously). But as someone who has survived your stage of life, I did learn a few things along the way.

In the following pages are stories, challenges, truths, and conversations to have. But before we jump into all of that, I have a request. Take out a pen and check the boxes beside things you have experienced so far in your life. Ready? Go!

- ☐ being afraid
- ☐ feeling pressure
- ☐ facing conflict with friends
- ☐ feeling insecure
- ☐ having disagreements with family

- ☐ dealing with a crush
- ☐ being stressed out
- ☐ comparing yourself to others
- ☐ having a question about God
- ☐ wanting a safe person to talk to about all of the above

Okay, let me guess. You checked at least five? Well, you're in good company. I have experienced all ten!

Throughout the following chapters, we're going to dive into all of these topics, and you'll have some great opportunities to learn about yourself, to learn about God, and to have helpful conversations with your mom (or whoever you're going through this book with).

It's our hope that you and your mom will have some meaningful conversations, develop a closer relationship, and have fun! You'll read the chapters written by me, and your mom will read the ones written by my mom.

Then there's the fun part! In the middle of the book, you'll find a section called "Meet Me in the Middle." Here, you and your mom will connect with questions and activities related to each topic. We want to help get the conversation going: maybe get you laughing, create some heart-to-heart discussion, and point you both to Scripture.

We'll talk a lot about viewing all the ups and downs of life through the lens of our faith. One of the passages we focus on throughout these pages is Philippians 4:4–9:

> **Rejoice** in the Lord always. I will say it again: Rejoice! Let your gentleness be evident to all. The Lord is near. Do not be anxious about anything, but in every situation, by prayer and petition, with thanksgiving, present your requests to God. And the peace of God, which transcends all understanding, will guard your hearts and your minds in Christ Jesus.
>
> Finally, brothers and sisters, whatever is true, whatever is noble, whatever is right, whatever is pure, whatever is lovely, whatever is admirable—if anything is excellent or praiseworthy—think about such things.

Whatever you have learned or received or heard from me, or seen in me—put it into practice. And the God of peace will be with you.

One of the reasons this Philippians passage is important is that it points to a package of characteristics that people who love Jesus should demonstrate.

In this book we'll talk about our hearts and our minds. Rejoicing, having a gentle spirit, not being anxious, dwelling on things that are honorable, right, pure, lovely, admirable, excellent, praiseworthy—these topics all make frequent appearances throughout the book. Why? Because what we dwell on—what we give attention to—impacts how we feel, think, and act.

You know this: When you spend your whole Saturday on the couch watching TV, you don't feel awesome. Maybe you are more irritable or sluggish because what you consumed all day was mindless and unhelpful. When you dwell on social media and constantly think about what other people are doing and how other people are "living their best lives," your thoughts may take you to a place you don't want to go, a place where you don't measure up and you are missing out. When you dwell on fitting in or being cool, you may find yourself acting in a way that doesn't align with who you know yourself to be.

What we dwell on is important. That's why we spend a lot of time throughout these pages dwelling on truths that will help you feel better, think more clearly, and act in a way that leads to the life you ultimately want.

So how do we do that? We begin by using a specific lens to view all of life, including all of our actions and decisions. That lens is the gospel.

The gospel is simply the *good news* of what Jesus did for you.

What exactly did Jesus do for you? I'm so glad you asked. I

could tell you, but I think it would make more sense coming from Jesus himself. In the book of John, Jesus perfectly explains God's good news for the world. Jesus says, "For God so loved the world that he gave his one and only Son, that whoever believes in him shall not perish but have eternal life" (John 3:16).

**Let's break this down.**

"For God so loved the world"—Before Jesus, humanity was separated from God because of sin. But because God loved you (you're part of the world), he wanted to do something about that.

**So what did he do?**

"He gave his one and only Son"—God sent Jesus to the world to live a perfect life and to beat sin as well as death by dying and coming back to life three days later. When humans sinned, a penalty needed to be paid. And Jesus paid it for us by dying on the cross.

**So what do we do?**

"Whoever believes in him shall not perish but have eternal life"—All we have to do is believe that Jesus is who he says he is. And that he did what he said he did! The reward is a real and everlasting relationship with him now and for eternity.

That is the gospel! That is the good news of what Jesus did for us! And it changes everything. It gives us a new lens for viewing life.

Because of that good news, we don't have to face the hard and frustrating parts of life alone. We don't have to live in our insecurities or our relational chaos or our stress or fear, because when Jesus died on the cross, he overcame all those things on our behalf.

So what does that kind of life look like? Keep reading to find out.

,

**Allie**

# CHAPTER 1

# Foundations Matter

Hi, my name is Allie, and I am a quitter. I have quit so many things. And I'm currently trying to quit quitting.

Two things about me you may find interesting: First, I don't like doing anything I am not good at. And second, I am not good at *a lot* of things. In my dream world, I'm amazing at something as soon as I start doing it. Like, so good I should give lessons. So when that doesn't happen, I quit. I'm not proud of it. Just being honest here.

Here's a noncomprehensive list of things I've started but quit because I wasn't immediately excellent at them:

1. Cross-stitch
2. Baking bread
3. Running
4. Candle-making
5. Basketball
6. Thrifting
7. Tennis
8. Knitting
9. Soccer
10. Golf

Believe it or not, there are more. But we don't have time to go through all of them. For now, notice number ten on the list. My husband, Clay, loves golf. And he's really good at it. So for his birthday this year I decided to go golfing with him. Now, I know what you're thinking: "Allie, just go and ride in the golf cart." Yes, I have been the golf-cart passenger princess in the past, and it's fun and all, but I decided I was going to be wife of the year by golfing *with* him.

So first things first: What to wear, right? I googled "What do you wear when you golf?" I didn't know a lot, but I did know golf has a dress code. The last thing I wanted was to give Clay the gift of embarrassment for his birthday. So I proceeded to buy a super-cute golfing outfit and immediately felt like this whole golf outing was going to be a huge success.

Next step, golf clubs. And no, I didn't go buy clubs. First of all, they were not in the budget. But also, I am self-aware enough at this point in my life not to spend hundreds of dollars on an activity that I am trying for the first time. I did need clubs though, so I found a friend who owned clubs but didn't care enough about them not to let me borrow them.

So far this was going *great*.

Then came the day. I packed snacks. I put on my cute golfy outfit. I shouldered the big golf bag that was as tall as me. And I stepped out onto the, uh, place where you start when you're doing golf.

Fast-forward to the end of what seemed like a *forever*-long day. Clay and I climbed back into his truck. I was sweating and sunburned and in all sorts of pain. I was also mad. Not mad at Clay. Just generally mad at the whole sport of golf. Why did I think that if I had the right outfit and the energy of a seven-month-old golden retriever puppy that I would go out there and be amazing at a sport that grown men spend their whole lives practicing just to be decent enough not to embarrass themselves?

Because I am me. It's what I do—thinking I'll be great at something on the first try.

I feel like you get the point. I want to be immediately incredible at everything I try to do. Unfortunately, that is not how life works.

Maybe you feel the same way. You want to be immediately awesome at whatever you do, and you aren't interested in putting in the time and effort it takes to be great. You wanted to join a team, but you didn't make the cut. Instead of training and practicing for the next year, you threw in the towel. You wanted to be an excellent cook, but when you burned round one, you gave up on the rest. You wanted to be awesome at a specific musical instrument, but practice got boring and you didn't seem to be getting better, so you decided to call it quits.

The truth is, being great at anything—a sport or musical instrument or some particular skill—takes practice.

Guess what? The same applies to our faith. We have to be intentional and consistent to grow our relationship with God. We don't just want to know *about* God. We want to know God personally. We want to have a relationship with God, through Jesus, that impacts not only our eternity but also how we live our lives. We want to make choices that help us move in the direction of a heavenly Father who loves us, a Savior who gave his life for us, and a helper who is in it with us!

Here is the key: to know God personally and grow in our faith consistently, we have to incorporate some foundational beliefs and practices into our lives.

One key foundational belief is that we are *not* on our own in our faith journey. You see, we have a helper. Not only *a* helper but *the* Helper. God is present *with us* through the Holy Spirit.

Who is the Holy Spirit, you ask? Well, after Jesus died on the cross and rose again three days later, he spent some time hanging out with his disciples. The disciples must have been ecstatic to be reunited with Jesus, but Jesus had to tell them something he knew they would receive as bad news, something they would not be happy about. Jesus shared that he was leaving. They wouldn't see him anymore. They wouldn't be spending their days together anymore.

Naturally, they were pretty upset. He was their leader, their Lord, the one they looked to for guidance, direction, and instruction. And he was going away. But Jesus knew something they didn't. Jesus informed them that it was better for them that he go. He assured them that they would not be abandoned, because God was about to send his Spirit to dwell with each disciple individually.

Here's why this is good news. Jesus was one guy. Jesus's leaving and sending the Holy Spirit means that no one has to wait their turn to talk to Jesus or to experience God. Each person individually now has access to God!

That means we don't have to be in his physical presence to be in his presence. We don't have to wait in line to receive his instructions. And we don't have to wait to be comforted, because the Holy Spirit is our comforter.

Still unsure? Read these passages about the Holy Spirit, and do two things: (1) Underline the passage that makes the most sense to you. (2) Underline every characteristic of the Holy Spirit you can find. Ready?

> **When** he, the Spirit of truth, comes, he will guide you into all the truth. He will not speak on his own; he will speak only what he hears, and he will tell you what is yet to come. **(JOHN 16:13)**

> **The** Helper, the Holy Spirit whom the Father will send in My name, He will teach you all things, and remind you of all that I said to you. **(JOHN 14:26 NASB)**

**I** will ask the Father, and he will give you another advocate to help you and be with you forever—the Spirit of truth. The world cannot accept him, because it neither sees him nor knows him. But you know him, for he lives with you and will be in you. **(JOHN 14:16–17)**

**You** will receive power when the Holy Spirit comes on you; and you will be my witnesses in Jerusalem, and in all Judea and Samaria, and to the ends of the earth. **(ACTS 1:8)**

In Galatians, Paul gives us a list of things we will see more of in our lives the more we lean into and depend on the Holy Spirit:

**The** fruit of the Spirit is love, joy, peace, forbearance [patience], kindness, goodness, faithfulness, gentleness and self-control. **(GALATIANS 5:22–23)**

Isn't that amazing? Want more joy? More peace? More self-control? All the things? Because of the Holy Spirit, these characteristics increase in our lives as we grow in our faith.

Here's a little encouragement for you: Don't give up! Even when following Jesus feels difficult, even when things aren't getting easier, even if you keep messing up, don't give up. The longer we follow Jesus, the closer we get to him and the more consistently we live out these incredible gifts God offers.

If you're new in your faith, or you feel discouraged because you don't think you're crushing the whole faith thing, just remember: growing in your faith takes time and consistency. We don't have to strive, and we don't have to be perfect. But it does take some intentionality on our part to stay close to God.

Here are a few foundational practices that have helped me in my journey with God.

First, *we learn*. We spend time reading the Bible, praying, listening to sermons, and using resources that teach us the truths of God's Word. Maybe we join a Bible study or a small group. In doing so, the Holy Spirit meets us and does the work of planting God's truth inside us.

Throughout this book, we give you some specific and helpful ways to lean in and learn from God for yourself. These chapters follow the flow of Philippians 4:4–9, where Paul writes,

**Rejoice** in the Lord always. I will say it again: Rejoice! Let your gentleness be evident to all. The Lord is near. Do not be anxious about anything, but in every situation, by prayer and petition, with thanksgiving, present your requests to God. And the peace of God, which transcends all understanding, will guard your hearts and your minds in Christ Jesus.

Finally, brothers and sisters, whatever is true, whatever is noble, whatever is right, whatever is pure, whatever is lovely, whatever is admirable—if anything is excellent or praiseworthy—think about such things. Whatever you have learned or received or heard from me, or seen in me—put it into practice. And the God of peace will be with you.

What would it look like for you to learn this Scripture passage? You could write it on a note card and keep it with you, you could commit to reading it every day while you are reading this book, or you could memorize it.

God speaks to us through Scripture and uses it to grow our faith by helping us learn more about him and his heart. So I want to encourage you to *learn*.

Second, *we apply*. This is the doing part! We start doing what Scripture says. We start making an effort to live out what we have learned. When we read the Bible and apply what it says, something amazing happens. Our attitudes and our actions change. Love and gentleness and patience flow out of us more and more. And even when it's hard, we obey what God says.

Again, throughout the next few chapters, we will take Philippians 4:4–9 and apply it to our lives. And we'll see how applying those truths to our lives can change us from the inside out.

And third, *we continue*. Sometimes the process of growing in our faith is slow and frustrating, but I promise that if you stick to it, you will see something crazy happen. You will be transformed. Following the ways of Jesus becomes a way of life. This doesn't mean your life will be easy or perfect, but you'll find that you aren't doing it alone. Our powerful God is *with you* through the presence of his Spirit. And as the truths of God's Word take root in your life, things begin to change.

I memorized bits and pieces of Philippians 4:4–9 throughout my middle school and high school years, and all these years later I still call it to mind in times of stress and fear. When I don't know what to do, I remember the truths from this passage and continue to apply them to my life.

You can learn and grow from any passage of Scripture. But throughout the next few weeks, Philippians 4:4–9 will be our go-to passage. My prayer is that you'll allow the Holy Spirit to use these verses to grow your faith and that you'll be drawn into a closer relationship with Jesus.

Okay, allow me to issue a challenge! As we launch into the next chapters of this book, would you consider spending intentional time with God? Like, regularly?

Have you been asking the question, How do I grow my faith? The answer is simple. How do you grow any relationship you have? You spend time with that person. You talk to that person. You do life alongside that person. And guess what? It's the same with God.

Some people call spending time with God *quiet time*. But it doesn't necessarily have to be quiet. It is simply *time set aside specifically to meet with God*. For some of us, this looks like waking up a little bit earlier to read the Bible and pray. For some, it may look like reading a devotional between classes to remind yourself in the middle of the day that God is with you and cares about you. Or for others it may be putting on a worship song right before bed and journaling about what God is doing in your life.

For me, spending time with God has looked different in various seasons of my life. When I was in middle school, I had a specific devotional that I read every morning and night. When I was in high school, I would read the Bible before I went to sleep and listen to worship music on my way to school. In college, I started journaling, which helped me keep track of all the ways God was moving in my life. These days I wake up early to journal and read my Bible while I drink my coffee.

The point is, there is no perfect formula. There is no right or wrong way. It's simply time spent with God. And the truth is that *God wants to spend time with you.*

Just as it takes intentionality to develop your friendships, it takes intentionality to spend time with God throughout your days. So what can you do over the course of reading this book to set aside time to connect with God?

Here are some things that might help you establish a routine:

- a cozy spot in your house
- a warm drink
- your Bible
- a journal and a pen
- a devotional book or maybe this book
- a mentor or a friend who checks in on you to see if you're being consistent in your time with the Lord (not a bossy,

annoying person but maybe someone who also is trying to grow in their faith)

When it comes to our time alone with God, he doesn't love us *because* we spend time with him. He wants to spend time with us *because* he loves us. He wants a real relationship with us, and he wants to show us how to love the people around us. He wants us to grow in our faith and in our practice of it.

That's exactly what our quiet times, or our times with God, are meant to accomplish: meeting with our heavenly Father regularly, allowing the Holy Spirit to move in our lives, and using Scripture to learn, apply, and continue in our faith.

Give it a try. It just might change your life!

# CHAPTER 2

# You Are Who *God* Says You Are

I am about to tell you a story that haunts me to this day.

When I was in the eleventh grade, I had a big crush on a guy in my theater class. He was tall and funny and was friends with everyone. I wanted to figure out a way to get him to notice me. I didn't know much about this guy, but one thing I knew to be true: he loved comic books. Not only did he love comic books, but he had a favorite superhero, and that superhero was the Green Lantern. Definitely a unique choice for a favorite superhero.

At sixteen years old, I had approximately zero knowledge about this superhero other than I was pretty sure he had a Ring Pop on his finger at all times. That all changed when I got the idea to learn everything I could about the Green Lantern so that I could impress this guy. That's right. With my own money, I bought comic books and dove into the strange world of the Green Lantern. I'm not kidding—I went all in. I learned so much. I remember failing a pre-calc test, but I memorized the entire Green Lantern oath in hopes that this guy would like me.

The worst part is, no matter how much time passes, I can't seem to shake this random information from my brain. Do I remember anything from my biology class? No. Can I rattle off every color lantern and what each one represents? I sure can! (Side note: If you ever meet me, please quiz me on Green Lantern trivia so I can put all this info to good use.)

I suppose there's a silver lining in this little embarrassment from my past. The Green Lantern trivia lodged in my brain serves as a reminder, to this day, that I have an unhealthy tendency to change myself to get people to like me. I'd love to tell you that this Green Lantern fiasco was a one-off event. I cannot.

In the sixth grade I tried out for cheerleading because I thought the people at my new school would like me if I was a cheerleader. In the eighth grade, I got a boyfriend because I thought my friends would think I was cool if I had a boyfriend. The examples go on and on, but when I think about it, I did all that because I didn't believe I was good enough as I was.

Have you ever felt that way?

Maybe you wish you were more athletic so you could make the team.

Maybe you wish you were funnier so you could make your friends laugh.

Maybe you wish you were better looking so people would admire you.

Maybe you wish you were smarter so you could make your parents proud.

There are a million examples, but take a second to think about it for yourself. I want you to fill in the following blank with what you are tempted to think about yourself:

I am not _____ enough.

Maybe it's smart, funny, tall, pretty, athletic, popular, cool, likable, fun . . . you name it!

The problem is, when you believe that something, or maybe more than one thing, should fill that blank, there are a few possible outcomes, all of them negative. Here are three things that can happen when you feel like you fall short:

## You Change

You decide you're going to be better. You work harder. You strive. You stay up late studying. You run yourself into the ground training for tryouts. You watch makeup and hair tutorials and spend all your money on trendy clothes. You change your personality depending on the people you are around. You talk differently around certain people. You try to change yourself so that you will be enough.

The problem is that one day you may wake up and not know who you are. You've jumped from situation to situation changing so many things about yourself that you are far away from who you actually are. Or you wake up one day and look in the mirror and have no idea who you are because you've tried so hard to be enough. Enough for your friends, enough for your family, enough for strangers, enough for yourself, and maybe even enough for God.

## You Pretend

Maybe you believe you won't ever be enough, but you surely don't want other people knowing that! So what do you do? You pretend. You pretend to be smart by cheating on tests. You pretend to be cool by being mean to others. You pretend not to care about things or you lie to convince the people around you that you are enough.

You build the perfect persona online to prove to others that you are enough, but deep down you don't believe you are.

The problem with constantly pretending is that your relationships will suffer. Dishonesty breaks relationships, but it's even deeper than that. If you are not fully known, you won't be fully loved. People may love who they think you are, but if they don't know you, how can they truly love you?

## You Lose Heart

Maybe you've tried it all and you've realized it's not working. You feel hopeless. You believe you will never be enough, and you've given up on trying. You walk around painfully aware of your shortcomings, and you can't shake the feeling that things will never get better. You feel embarrassed and insecure, and you believe this is how you'll always feel.

The problem is that walking around hopeless is so far from the abundant life you were created to live, the abundant life God has for you.

When we don't feel like we are enough, we work to change ourselves, or we pretend, or we lose heart. And none of these options are good ones.

What if I told you that no matter where you fall in these three categories, there is a better way? What if it's true that regardless of where you fall on those lists of things we tend to use as standards, you can be just fine? Better than fine, actually.

For that to be the case, here's the question we need to ask: Who am I?

You may think, "Well, I am a lot of things . . ."

I'm a friend.
I'm a student.
I'm a daughter.
I'm a sister.
I'm a teammate.

Hear me out. These are *roles* you have. You have a lot of roles, and they play a part in making up who you are. But I want to go deeper than that. I want to look at the root of who you are: your identity.

Typically, when it comes to feeling like we're not enough, our identity is what suffers. We believe that because we're not ____ enough, we're not valuable, we're not lovable. Maybe we feel like our lives have no point.

What if I told you that your true value is based not on your behavior or the approval of others but on *what God says is true of you*? And here we encounter a big truth about him. It's made clear to us in the very first chapter of the very first book of the Bible.

*He made us.* God made us in his own image, in his likeness (Genesis 1:26–27). And he gave humankind purpose. That purpose was to reflect God wherever we go. God created humanity to have purpose and fulfillment and hope as they experienced fellowship with him and reflected him to the world around them.

But *we sinned* and broke the relationship. Purpose and fulfillment broke too. And along with all that, we got confused about our image. We mistakenly began looking elsewhere for purpose and value and worth. We started changing in our effort to find significance, and pretending in order to be worthy, and losing heart when it all fell apart.

Then *we were restored* to his image through Christ's death, resurrection, and payment for our sin. "Because of his great love for us, God, who is rich in mercy, made us alive with Christ even when we were dead in our transgressions—it is by grace you have been saved" (Ephesians 2:4–5). We didn't deserve this grace, nor did we earn it. He just chose to give it. He gave it by redeeming us from our sin and our brokenness through the death and resurrection of his only Son, Jesus.

Think about this. When God looks at you, he doesn't see a *cleaned-up version* of sinful you, or even a forgiven version of the you who is trying to do better. He sees you as his redeemed daughter. A brand-new creation with no scars, no spots, and no blemishes left over from your past. Your value to him is off the charts, and you don't have to perform. You don't have to earn *anything*.

And now *he gives us purpose*. That's right, he has given us back our purpose and paved the way to fulfillment and hope! Through the power of the Holy Spirit in us, we are to be God's image bearers every day, reflecting his character (love), his fruit (love, joy, peace, patience, kindness, goodness, gentleness, faithfulness, and self-control), and his ways to the world around us.

We don't just arrive at that destination though, right? For these truths to transform us, we have to take some intentional steps. I have a few suggestions, of course!

## Keep Truth in Front of You

Renewing our minds is an ongoing process. The culture we live in, the patterns and habits we've established over time, and the careless words of others (by accident or on purpose) all conspire daily to derail us from remembering who we are in Christ.

Our quiet time is a super-important defense against those lies. So is memorizing Scripture verses or having them in our line of sight throughout the day—as wallpapers on our screens, under a magnet on the fridge, on note cards where we can see them, or on sticky notes attached to our bathroom mirror. Personally, I am a huge sticky-note-on-the-bathroom-mirror girl. In high school, I wanted to break up with my boyfriend, and it took quite a few empowering sticky notes on my mirror to hype me up enough to do it. Trust me when I say sticky notes on a mirror have power.

Spend a little time thinking about the best way to keep truth in front of you. Consider the routines and rhythms of your normal day. Where can you put important truths of who you are that you will see every day?

## Live Out Your Identity

In the following chapters, we'll talk about all kinds of ways we can fully embrace our identity and reflect God's image to the world around us. It's one thing to know our value and our worth and another to live like it. For now, let's take a look at our Philippians passage. It's full of practical ways to live out who God says we are:

**Rejoice** in the Lord always. I will say it again: Rejoice! Let your gentleness be apparent to all. The Lord is near. Be anxious for nothing, but in everything, by prayer and petition, with thanksgiving, present your requests to God. And the peace of God, which surpasses all understanding, will guard your hearts and your minds in Christ Jesus.

Finally, brothers, whatever is true, whatever is honorable, whatever is right, whatever is pure, whatever is lovely, whatever is admirable—if anything is excellent or praiseworthy—think on these things. Whatever you have learned or received or heard from me, or seen in me, put it into practice. And the God of peace will be with you. **(PHILIPPIANS 4:4–9 BSB)**

In this passage, Paul paints a picture of what it looks like to live out your identity. Several "to-do" gems are buried in these verses:

- **Rejoice.** Even when our circumstances seem bleak, there is power in rejoicing. Not pretending to *like* the circumstances, but rejoicing in the **truth** that God is with us in them. This is a way we can live out our true identity.

- **Be gentle.** When difficult situations catch us off guard, our knee-jerk response isn't usually gentleness. At least mine isn't. But if we pause and remind ourselves of the **truth** that God is with us, and in us, we can take a deep breath and respond with gentleness.. This is a way we can live out our true identity.

- **Pray.** Many Scriptures throughout the Bible point to the **truth** that God hears us when we pray. No prayer is unheard or not responded to by God. He will never ignore us. A posture of prayer is an invitation for our heavenly Father to meet us, to meet *with* us, and to whisper his affirmation and purpose into our souls.. This is a way we can live out our true identity.

- **Dwell on the good stuff.** Paul just outlined what a bunch of the good things are. He lists them so we can take them in and begin to dwell on them and allow the **truth** of their goodness to transform us. He tells us to dwell on them because he knows our minds are where lies so easily take root. As we dwell more and more on the good replacements, those lies are dug up and thrown out. This is a way we can live out our true identity.

So to wrap up all this good news: God loves you, he chose you, and you have a purpose here on earth. You are a child of the God of the universe! You don't have to change, you don't have to pretend, and you don't need to lose heart. All of this is true not because you were good enough but because God loved you from the start without you ever having to change or pretend. I know—amazing! So what does this mean for you?

**To the changer:** God made you on purpose for a purpose. This means you don't have to change yourself to be enough. Because of what Jesus did for you, you are *already* enough.

**To the pretender:** God fully knows you, intentionally chose you, and deeply loves you. You can be who God created you to be because you know God loves *you*. You don't have to pretend anymore.

**To the hopeless:** There is hope for you. Jesus died for you and loves you. You can be sure that you are enough. Through a relationship with Jesus, you can have hope on this side of eternity and on the other side. In other words, God has given you eternal life after this one *and* a plan for your life now—one filled with purpose and meaning.

Because of what Jesus did on the cross, you can know:

You are valuable.
You are loved.
You are enough.

So now that we know who we are, let's live it out!

CHAPTER 3

# No Win in Comparison

Have you ever forgotten whether you brushed your teeth? No, for real. Can you remember brushing your teeth this morning? I'm not accusing you of *not* brushing your teeth or being gross. But because I brush my teeth every single day, I can't always remember the specifics.

The reason I don't always remember is because, for me, and hopefully for you too, brushing my teeth is second nature. Things we do all the time often become second nature: playing sports, typing, doing dance routines, singing songs we know, driving the route to school, etc. When we do something enough, we don't have to think very hard about it.

*Second nature* is defined as "a characteristic or habit in someone that appears to be instinctive because that person has behaved in a particular way so often."[12]

When you do something so much, you don't even have to think about it. If you play a sport or an instrument or have a hobby, it often becomes second nature. This can be a good thing. But bad habits can become second nature too.

Anyone bite their nails? Anyone habitually drop clothes on the floor? Anyone let certain words slip out that could cause your grandma to spit out her tea?

Don't worry, we're not talking about hygiene or cussing in this chapter. We're talking about something far more discreet and yet extremely detrimental. We're talking about *comparison*—specifically, comparing ourselves to other people.

There are two types of people in this world:

- people who know comparison is a problem for them
- people who don't know comparison is a problem for them because it's second nature

Throughout my life, I have often thought of the second-nature habit of comparison as a game.

---

## The Comparison Game

### Objective
Simple: to discover how you are doing in life.

### Instructions
Players must measure themselves against the people around them using unrealistic expectations, social media, and unreasonably high standards.

### Rules
- Player must compare their worst days to their opponents' best days.
- Player must completely lose sight of all the good things in their lives.

- Player must lose at least two nights of sleep over a made-up conversation in their head that other people are having about them.

## Bonus Points

+3 points if the person a player compares themselves to most frequently is in their own family.

+3 points every time a player says something mean about someone as a result of comparison.

## How to Win

A player will be declared the winner of the game of comparison when they reach total dissatisfaction in life and lose their grip on all contentment.

---

Sound fun? Not really.

**The** truth is, everyone plays the comparison game, and everyone loses.

When I was in middle school, I realized that comparison was a problem for me. Because I was homeschooled in elementary school, entering middle school was quite a shock. Something else that shocked me: quizzes. We didn't have those at home. I didn't even know what quizzes were. My mom didn't teach me about those, and up until that point I knew only things that my mom knew. So when this mysterious paper was placed in front of me, I skimmed it, answered a few questions here and there, and gave it back to my teacher. I got . . . wait for it . . . a 10. Not a 10/10 or even a 10/20. No. No, I got a 10/100.

I should have been deeply embarrassed, right? I wish. Because

I was unfamiliar with the concept of a quiz, I loosely talked about my 10 until a very honest (a.k.a. mean) girl informed me that I was a moron. That's right. In that moment, I fell headlong into the trap of comparison.

For quite a while these stinging thoughts echoed through my sixth-grade brain: "She is smart. You are dumb. She is better. You are worse."

That's my first real memory of comparison. While I'm sure it had happened before, that was the instance that made a deep impression. It stands out in my mind. I was playing the comparison game and I was *losing*. I wish I could tell you it stopped there. But sadly, that was only the beginning of my comparison journey.

The interesting thing about comparison is that sometimes it makes you feel good. Sometimes when we compare, we end up coming out on top. We are the ones calling the new girl in school a moron. Okay, maybe we don't actually say that, because we're nicer than that mean girl. Oh shoot, I'm doing it again. But our thoughts trend in that direction when we feel *better than*.

When I was in high school, I learned that I did really well in my English class. I was making better grades than some of my smartest friends. That comparison made me feel good about myself. But it still wasn't helpful. When you compare yourselves to others, there are two possible outcomes:

## 1. You Become Envious

If you compare and feel less than, you become envious.

Envy simply means you want what the other person has.

In high school, I did theater. Let me tell you that theater auditions are literally soaked with comparison. How could they not be? The point of them is to sing *better*, dance *better*, act *better*, look *better* than the competition. So every time I didn't get the part I wanted, I was envious of the girl who did. I wasn't happy with the part I got. I was upset that I didn't get the part she got.

When you become envious, you tend to look right past the things you have and focus on the things you don't have. This is a problem because it causes you to neglect all the good things about yourself and to grow sad and discontent.

And it makes friendships really hard.

## 2. You Become Superior

If you compare and feel better than, you become superior.

Feeling superior simply means you put yourself above someone else. In your mind, you're better than they are. Does that sound familiar?

"Okay, maybe I didn't do great on that test, but at least I did better than him."

"Sure, maybe I shouldn't have made that choice, but at least I don't do what those people do."

"I could be much worse. I could be like them . . ."

In English class I started to brag: "What did you get on your paper? Oh, you got an 85? I got a 97!" I diminished the people around me because I was finally on top!

When we feel superior, we shut others down to make ourselves feel better. That may make us feel better in the moment, but it leads to broken relationships and false confidence.

*So what do we do?*

Well, first, we can't have this conversation without truly understanding the previous chapter.

Let me tell you, you can't beat the comparison game until

you fully realize and accept your identity as a loved and cherished daughter of God. Your value doesn't come from how other people see you or from how you measure up to others. Your value comes from the fact that Jesus went to the cross for you.

**Comparison says:** Fix your eyes on the people around you.
**Culture says:** Fix your eyes on yourself.
**God says:** Fix your eyes on Jesus.

Fixing our eyes on Jesus changes everything. It changes how we view ourselves. It changes how we view the people around us. And it sets us up to break out of the trap of comparison.

The author of Hebrews gives us an important instruction: "Let us run with perseverance the race marked out for us" (12:1). This paints a picture in my head of a running track. We each have an individualized track given to us by God.

You have a track.

Your friend has a track.

That social media influencer has a track.

That famous athlete has a track.

Your mom has a track.

Everyone has a different track and a different race they are running. Yours is special and unique *to you*. Your friend's is special and unique *to her*.

**God** made you *exactly* the way you are so you could run the race he set just for you.

That's why you don't have to compare races. You don't need to compare speed. You don't need to compare purposes. You don't need to compare your talents or your looks or your reputation. You need to fix your eyes on Jesus and run the race he has for *you*.

The author of this passage knew that sometimes things get in the way and keep us from running our race effectively. Have you ever run with a backpack on? You know what I'm talking about: You're late to class, so you have to run. Your backpack is bouncing up and down, tugging at your back and shoulders. Honestly, it feels ridiculous to me. If you're an Olympic backpack runner, congratulations. That is amazing. But for me, running with a backpack on feels super awkward.

I ask you this because the author of Hebrews says, "Let us throw off everything that hinders and the sin that so easily entangles" (12:1). The author knew that running with a backpack on majorly slows us down. There are metaphorical things he wants us to take off to run our race as best we can.

Two categories of things slow us down and make us less effective in the race God has called us to run:

1. Everything that hinders.
2. The sin that so easily entangles.

Let's tackle the sin that entangles first. These are the obvious things that you know God doesn't want for you. They are probably things you and your mom have talked about before. Or things you've discussed if you're in a small group or Bible study. These are things like gossip, lying, stealing, cheating, pride, disobedience, sexual immorality, etc. Those are the obvious things that keep you from running your race well.

The second category—or actually the first category, since I flipped them—is everything that hinders. These things aren't necessarily sin but can still keep you from running your race successfully. Something in this category could be a friendship or relationship that isn't pushing you to be the best version of yourself. It could be a habit that's taking up time that you could spend doing something better. Or it could simply be something that distracts you from doing what you know God is calling you to do.

I think comparison is a huge hindrance. The author of Hebrews is telling you to throw this off. Throw it away. Get it out of here! And get back to running your race more easily and effectively.

So how do we do this? I would like to suggest two things:

1. Celebrate what God has given others.
2. And leverage what God has given you.

## Celebrate What God Has Given Others

When you feel envious, celebrate others. Oof. This will probably be a highly unnatural thing to do, at least at first. According to my mom, "Celebrating other people diminishes jealousy's power over you." If you don't want to be controlled by jealousy, take the intentional and difficult step of celebrating the person you're jealous of.

Ideally, do it out loud and *to that person*:

- When your friend gets asked out on *another* date, go over and help her get ready. Follow up and listen to how it went. Be there for her and encourage her, even when you wish it were you.
- When your classmate makes a better grade than you even though you studied harder, be happy for her and tell her you're proud of her.
- When someone makes the team or gets the part you wanted, pass them a note saying congratulations and that you'll be cheering them on.

Celebrating others not only helps your relationships but also helps your own heart. It's hard. It's a choice. But I promise it's better than gossiping, rolling your eyes, or harboring resentment in your heart.

## Leverage What God Has Given You

What has God given you that you can use to help others? When you leverage what God has given you, you're able to influence others in a good way.

- You typically make better grades than that one friend? Instead of feeling superior, leverage your knowledge to help her get a better grade.
- You're one of the best players on the team? Volunteer to help someone improve. Stay after school or after practice, and use your influence to make someone else better.

Instead of allowing comparison to make you feel better than others,

- Identify what you're great at.
- Thank God for giving you that gift.
- Seek influence and help the people around you by leveraging your strengths.

We've looked over Philippians 4:4–9 quite a few times, but I want to pick it apart piece by piece to apply the truths to our lives. So what truth from this passage will help us quit the comparison game?

In Philippians 4:4, Paul says, "Rejoice in the Lord always. I will say it again: Rejoice!" I like that he says it twice. He knows it can be incredibly difficult, which is why I hear Paul say, "It feels like you didn't hear me the first time, so I'll say it again. *Rejoice! Just do it!*"

Another way to say rejoice is "Be glad!" No matter where you fall when you compare, you can choose to be glad. You didn't make the team? Be glad for the people who did! It's hard. But the more you do it, the easier it gets. You got a better grade on a presentation than your friend? Instead of feeling superior, offer to partner up and help the next time a project like that comes around. You feel bad about yourself because you don't look a certain way? Look in the mirror and pick two things about yourself to be glad about! You feel trapped in the comparison game? Look to Jesus and be glad you have him to lean on and learn from.

When you come up less than, instead of allowing insecurity to overtake you, rejoice. And celebrate others.

When you come up better than, instead of allowing pride to overtake you, rejoice. And leverage what God has given you.

As you celebrate others and leverage what God has given you, fix your eyes on Jesus. Not on the people around you. Not on yourself. On *Jesus*. Remember what he did for you, and rejoice in the race he has set for you. Just you. Your unique race. There is no better way to break out of the comparison game!

CHAPTER 4

# Family Is Forever

On September 20, 2019, the man of my dreams got down on one knee on the dock of my parents' lake house and asked me to marry him. Honestly, I think I blacked out, because I don't remember that moment. I have seen a lot of pictures, and people promise me that it happened. Also, we're married now.

That set into motion a wild seven months of trying to have an opinion on random things like the color of ink on invitations and what shade of white paper that ink would be printed on. Pardon me for thinking white was enough of a color. Nope. I learned there are approximately seven hundred shades of white paper, and I'm pretty sure my mom made me look at all seven hundred.

Let's just say that season was a lot of work.

Here's a little something about my mom. She loves making lists, being organized, staying ahead, and creating perfection. I love that about her, but I did not inherit those traits from her. I have the uncanny ability to sit back, relax, and trust that everything will work itself out. (PS: It's easy to trust that everything is going to work out when 99 percent of the time it's your mom who makes it all work out.)

Long story short, my mom and I spent months and months planning the perfect wedding. Here was the plan. First, we would invite every person we had ever come into contact with. Second, we would have food so delicious that everyone would talk about it at every wedding they would ever attend. And third, everyone would cry because of how beautiful our love was. Sounded like a good plan to me!

It was all set. Our wedding date: April 4, 2020 (4-4-2020). How cute, right?

Well, let's just say, Clay and I did not end up getting married on that day. And no, we didn't have a big fight and break our engagement. Here's what happened. Three weeks before the big day, the president addressed the nation and told us that we were entering a global pandemic. Ever heard of Covid? Yep, that.

That announcement kicked off a few weeks of chaos and tears. My mom and I had to slowly release all the plans and dreams we had for my wedding. First, we cut the guest list from five hundred to one hundred. Okay, okay. That wasn't *so* terrible. I didn't need my mom's chiropractor to come anyway.

But then a day later, we needed to cut it to seventy-five. Ouch. Looked like my favorite babysitter was out too. Another day later, we lost the venue. I told myself not to panic. We could get married in a backyard?

And another day later, I got a call from my mom. "I am so sorry to do this, Allie, but we have to make a choice. Either you can have your bridal party or your grandparents at your wedding. We can't risk exposing your grandparents to this sickness."

That was the breaking point for me. I don't have sisters, so the women in my bridal party were the closest I had to sisters in my life. I knew I was going to choose my grandparents, but each phone call to one of my friends telling them they couldn't stand next to me on this extremely important day broke my heart. By the time

I had gotten through the list, I was sobbing on a curb outside my almost-in-laws' house. It was a low moment.

I didn't care about the cake or the invitations or even the dress (which I hadn't picked up yet—yikes!). I cared about the people who were no longer going to be there. That I was going to have the most momentous moment of my life without my closest friends was devastating to me. Then that sadness turned to something else. Desperation? Insanity? I'm not sure, but in that moment, after so much had been taken away from my wedding, I refused to allow anything else to be taken away.

Clay and I decided to get married *that day*.

Before anything else fell through the cracks. Before the thirty-seven people who could still come could no longer come. The governor was considering whether we would "shelter in place" for two weeks. I didn't know exactly what that meant, but I did know it would eliminate all chances of any wedding at all!

I called my parents and declared, "Clay and I are getting married *today*."

Of course, my sweet mother panicked. "Allie, just give me twenty-four hours. We can still make this great."

Deal.

I then proceeded to call my photographer and videographer and said, "You doing anything tomorrow?" The rest of that day was a blur of activity, but the next day I was standing in the same place where Clay proposed to me. With my family surrounding me, I committed my life to my best friend. Clay and I were married.

Why do I tell you this story? Because friendships are so important. God made us to be in community. But family? *Family is forever.* Family is the group of people God designed to be in your life for all of life. To celebrate you. To cry with you. To be there in the highs and the lows.

We didn't dance a lot at my wedding, but one of my three

dances was with my grandfather. In that moment, I knew beyond a shadow of a doubt that I'd made the right choice.

Family is forever. Family is where you come from. And family is crazy important.

But sometimes family relationships can also be really hard.

Family looks different for everybody. But the truth remains: family is important. Believe it or not, your family shapes who you are and even what you believe to be true about yourself. Family even creates the roles you have in this world. You're a daughter. You're a granddaughter. Maybe you're a sister or a cousin or a niece. Family dictates some parts of who we actually are!

If family is so important though, why are family relationships sometimes the most complicated ones we have? They can be messy and difficult and frustrating.

- Maybe you have an older sibling who is mean to you or a younger one who bothers you beyond all understanding.
- Maybe you have a sibling or a close cousin who's making decisions you know are hurting them.
- Maybe you have a parent who always seems angry, and you wonder if it's partly your fault.
- Maybe you have a mom or dad who left, and feeling abandoned is the worst.
- Maybe you split your time between family members' houses, and you always feel unsettled.
- Maybe you have a family member who passed away, and life feels lonely without them.
- Maybe you have grandparents who live with you, and your home always feels crowded.
- Maybe you have grandparents you don't know at all, and you can't help but wonder what the real story is.

In your season of life, there are a lot of things you *can't* choose about your family. You didn't get to choose them to start with. Also, you have no control over the decisions they make. And that's hard sometimes.

So for the next few minutes I want to walk you through a few things you *can* choose when it comes to your family.

## 1. You Can Choose to Appreciate Your Family

First, you can choose to appreciate your family. No matter what your family looks like, or the decisions that have been made, those decisions have made you. The reason you are on this earth is because God used your parents, and their choices, to bring you here. Even if you are adopted, you can look back at your birth family and be thankful they did what they did to get you here.

You can look at your family and appreciate what they do for you.

- Do your parents work hard to provide for you and your family financially? That's something to appreciate.
- Does your family make sure you are fed and clothed and get to school so that you can have a bright future? That's something to appreciate.
- Does someone in your family do laundry? Let me tell you, as someone who has to do her own laundry now, I think *that* is something to appreciate.
- What about food? Does someone make sure there are groceries in the house? That's something to appreciate.
- When you take a shower, is there soap in there? Somebody put it there. That's something to appreciate.
- Do you have inside jokes or ways of saying things that no one but your siblings get? That's something to appreciate.

- Does your older brother or sister, as irritating as it might be, want to protect you? That's something to appreciate.

Look at your family through the lens of appreciation, and I promise that your negative attitude, and even some of the frustrations you experience, may fade a little bit.

My dad always says, "Unexpressed gratitude is experienced as ingratitude." Meaning, it's one thing to be thankful for your family, but it's another thing to tell them or show them you are thankful for them. So here's what I want you to do. Make a list on your phone, or on a sticky note, of every time you see a family member do something you appreciate. Then when the note is full, find a time to go to them and read off everything you appreciate about them. This will make their day and bring you closer together. Give it a try!

## 2. You Can Choose to Forgive Your Family

We know that no person is perfect. And families are little groups of imperfect people. Therefore, family members are going to hurt each other. Whether intentionally or unintentionally, family members will hurt, embarrass, frustrate, annoy, upset, and maybe even scar us at one point or another. And isn't it true that the people closest to us can do the most damage?

Parents, even when they mean well, can say or do things that cut deeply. They sometimes embarrass us or hurt our feelings, but they have no idea.

So what can you do? Well, there are really only two options: You can hold on to your anger. Or you can let go of your anger. In other words, you get to choose *to forgive* or *not to forgive*.

Let's head down the "not forgiving" road for a second, shall we? Holding on to anger feels good. It feels justified. It feels powerful.

Sometimes it even feels right, or righteous. Here's what it often looks like:

**Having imaginary conversations with that person.** You know those conversations. The ones in your head. The ones where you say the perfect thing and they have no comeback? Yeah, those.

**Talking poorly about them to other people.** When someone treats us poorly, even if it's someone in our family, we naturally want to tell everyone. We want everyone to agree that they are bad and we are good. We want everyone on *our* side.

**Ignoring them.** In other words, we go quiet. We emotionally drop them without a word. As a way of punishing them, we act like they don't exist.

**Blowing up at them.** Maybe for some of you, you get into an actual full-on fight. Whether in person or over text, we may be tempted to tell them exactly how we feel and to try to hurt them the way they hurt us.

But here's the problem. *When you hold on to anger, anger holds on to you.*

When you're angry and refuse to do the work required to forgive, you may feel powerful and in control, but the reality is that ugliness has a grip on you. Your mind automatically drifts to that imaginary conversation. When someone brings that person up, you immediately launch into the whole story and rehash it. You have less control over your anger than you think you do.

What is wrong with that? You were deeply hurt, so why is it bad to be mad forever?

There's a common saying that is so true: "Resentment [not forgiving someone] is like drinking poison and expecting the other person to die."

Holding on to rage and grudges and anger will hurt only you. It takes up your brain space. It makes you bitter. It hurts your other relationships too. Ultimately you are trapped. Who wants to be trapped by their own anger?

Forgiveness, on the other hand, is powerful. It untraps us. It frees us. And, most importantly, it's one of the clearest pictures of what being a Jesus follower looks like. Jesus forgave us, and he asks us to do the same for people who hurt us. But Jesus took forgiveness to the next level, and he asks us to do the same. We're not just to forgive and walk away. *We are to restore.* It's harder. In our inner-circle relationships, especially our family relationships, we are to take the next step of restoring the broken relationship. Mental forgiveness is only the first step. It's only half the equation.

Think about this: Jesus was not content only to forgive. God's forgiveness, through what Jesus did for us on the cross, was a means to an end. *Restoring* the broken relationship was what was most important to him.

Jesus commanded us to do for others what he did for us: "In your relationships with one another, have the same mindset as Christ Jesus" (Philippians 2:5). What was his mindset? Forgiveness and restoration. There are a lot of ways to restore broken relationships. And some relationships that fracture need forgiveness and restoration without necessarily being close again. Relationships need to have healthy boundaries. That's definitely something to talk about with your mom or a trusted adult. But usually when it comes to family, restoration and renewed closeness are the goal.

When I need to forgive, I use the four Rs:

**Recognize:** Who do I need to forgive?
**Release:** Actually forgive. This can be face-to-face, or sometimes it can be on your own. I prefer a dramatic forgiveness moment that will stick with me. I write everything out in

my journal. I write who did it, what they did, and how it made me feel. Then I take a deep breath and, with a marker, write over the entire page "FORGIVEN." You could also write it out, crumple it up, and throw it in the garbage or fire! Regardless of how you do it, it's important to have a specific moment when you forgive the person who has wronged you.

**Remember:** Walk in that forgiveness. You may wake up the next day and be tempted to fall back into your old ways of anger and bitterness. But forgiveness is not a feeling, it's a choice. So regardless of how you feel, you can look back and remember that what that person did is no longer something you hold against them because you have already chosen to forgive.

**Restore:** What conversation needs to happen to get your relationship back on solid footing?

## 3. You Can Choose Gentleness When It Comes to Your Family

You can also choose gentleness. Gentleness? Like walking barefoot through a field of daisies? Eh, not really. I am talking about gentleness in the ways you speak and act: what you say, how you say it, what you do, how you do it.

I grew up with two older brothers, and when they picked on me, being gentle seemed like it would make me look weak. If they yelled, I needed to yell louder. If they were rude, I needed to be ruder. If they slammed a door, I needed to slam it harder. But being less gentle than my brothers never really got me anywhere. It mostly got me into trouble and made everyone even more angry.

I remember one day my mom looked at me and said, "Allie,

your reaction is what they're looking for, you know?" No, I did not know. A part of the fun for my brothers was to get me angry, to get me loud, and to get me upset. So I decided to take a different approach.

The louder they got, the quieter I became. The meaner they got, the kinder I tried to be. The more worked up they got, the gentler I decided to be. Want to know what happened? It was a lot less exciting for them to pick on me. When they started getting "gentle Allie," they no longer had the satisfaction of getting me worked up. And then they would end up feeling guilty for being mean. Mission accomplished. It turns out, gentleness was the best weapon I could use to put them in their place.

Was putting them in their place the ultimate goal? Of course not. But once I stopped allowing them to have control over my reactions, I learned that gentleness was a superpower.

Philippians 4:5 says, "Let your gentleness be evident to all." We know what *all* means. It means your sister. It means your brother. It means your dad. It means your mom. It means *all*.

One of the ways we can be gentle is in our speech. When we are irritated with our siblings, instead of calling them a garbage face (or whatever your go-to insult is), we can take a deep breath and calmly ask them to stop what they are doing. When we are mad at our mom or dad for not letting us do something we want to do, instead of mouthing off, we can choose gentleness and say, "Okay."

Want to know when I am least likely to be gentle? When I'm *hungry*. That sounds simplistic, but I am a firm believer that the Holy Spirit works through me much better when I am well fed. My least gentle moments were after school when I would get in the car with my mom or one of my brothers, and I was ready to unleash my hunger rage. An easy fix? I started keeping an after-school snack with me. I kid you not, that made all the difference.

Family relationships can be messy. We don't choose our family.

We can't control our family. But there are things we *can* control. We *can* choose to appreciate. We *can* choose to forgive. We *can* choose to be gentle.

If you take only one thing from this whole chapter, here it is: when it comes to figuring out how to be gentle with your family, sometimes you just need to eat a snack.

# CHAPTER 5

# Finding Your People

Few things have impacted my faith more than one particular decision I made when I was a sophomore in high school. Want to know what it was? I decided to lead a middle school small group. That's right, fifteen-year-old me filled out a form, stumbled through an interview, and then was handed ten to thirty-two middle school girls to lead on Sunday mornings. Side note: Two adults led the group with me; my church wasn't that reckless.

Throughout my three years of leading that group of girls, I learned what it meant to lead. I learned about having hard conversations. I learned the importance of showing up for people and walking alongside younger girls who were going through things that were way above my pay grade. I truly loved these girls, and over time I realized I was holding myself to a higher standard *because of them.*

When I faced difficult choices with boys or friends, a little question would pop into my head: "Will this decision tempt you to lie to your middle school girls?" I never wanted to lie to them about the decisions I was making. And that pushed me to make better decisions.

At the end of my senior year, which was their eighth-grade

year, I knew these girls were about to launch into high school. I started thinking of all that was ahead of them and what they would face. I loved them so much, and the thought of leaving them behind as I headed out of state to college was hard. They'd be braving the world of high school without me. So I decided to make a list. Some might call it a list of rules, but to me it is a list of everything I learned in high school that I wanted to share with my girls. The cute things and the ugly things. The things I learned through watching friends. And the things I personally learned the hard way.

So, ladies, here is a shortened version of that list I want to share with you. Why? Because just like I loved and cared for them, I love and care about you!

1. Surround yourself with people who build you up, not people who tear you down.
2. Treat your kisses like you have a limited supply.
3. Guard your heart. Seriously . . . your heart is precious.
4. Stay vertical. Set your physical boundaries and stick to them.
5. Have an accountability partner and be willing to tell HER everything.
6. Be so so so so so so so SO SO SO SO careful about who you date.
7. If you're wondering if you should break up with him, break up with him.
8. If your girl gets broken up with, go buy her a stuffed animal, a blanket, candy, and lots and lots of ice cream. (Other gifts are acceptable too.)
9. Pray, PRAY, PRAY! Don't ever forget how much you need God.
10. Have a quiet time. It may seem like a hassle, but it will help you stay close to God.

11. Be nice to your parents. They love you and want the best for you, so if you disagree with them, just realize that they are a lot smarter than you . . . sorry about it.

12. If you find yourself lying to your parents or other adults in your life, backtrack and get out of that situation IMMEDIATELY. You are somewhere you do not want to be.

13. Never be afraid to say no. It's better to be a wimp than dead.

14. When you fall on your face, get back up and keep moving (literally and figuratively).

15. Journal so you can look back and see what God has done in your life.

16. Even when you don't want to, GO TO CHURCH!

17. If it's not classy, don't do it.

18. Don't judge. Even when people are doing things you don't agree with, show them love.

19. Pause before you speak . . . this will prevent a lot of problems.

20. Selfies are for faces.

Some of these are funny but true. Some are serious and also true. A few are warnings meant to keep you safe and happy. None of these are meant to keep you from enjoying high school or having fun; they are simply meant as boundaries to help you have the best high school experience ever.

What's funny is that most of these fall into two categories: friends and boys.

I wasn't super popular in high school. I wasn't drowning in friends and friend drama. I also wasn't super boy crazy. Actually, let me think about that statement, because I never want to lie to you . . . Okay, it's true. I really don't think I was *that* boy crazy. Even so, these two categories, friends and boys, were almost always on my mind. They were a big deal for me, and I'm sure they're a big deal for you too. So let's talk about them!

What I know about these relationships, or any relationships really, is that each relationship has three potential stages:

- before you get close
- while you are close
- when you are no longer close

Of course, some friendships and relationships last forever. But for those that don't, it is important to be equipped to handle relationships well in each stage. I'll tell you a little secret: no matter what stage of a relationship you are in, you are called to *love*.

So let's jump in.

## Before You Get Close

The first stage is before you get close. *Close* is a relative term. This could mean before you start dating, when you're thinking about making the relationship official, or when you are just realizing you might *like like* them. For a friendship, this could be when you meet a new person and discover you have things in common. You realize you might want to get to know them better. Maybe you start inviting them to events, having more meaningful conversations, and getting to know them on a deeper level.

The people you allow yourself to be close to will influence your life. That's true for all of us. The people we're closest to have an effect on us. They subtly pull us in certain directions. These can be good directions or bad. So in this season of the relationship, it's important to figure out which way the relationship could go.

Here are some important questions to ask yourself:

- What kind of friends do I want to have?
- What are the characteristics of good friendships?
- What makes a lifelong friend?
- What causes friendships to be short term, and how do I avoid those?
- Is this a person I'd like to introduce to my parents and my siblings?

Whether it's a friendship or a relationship with a boy, all these questions apply. But the next one might be the most important of all.

- Do I want to be more like this person?

Regardless of whether we choose to move closer to a person, God calls us to a certain standard in our relationships. We are to care for, and love well, all the people he puts in our paths. In 1 Corinthians 13, Paul lays out a clear picture of *perfect* love. This is the love God has for us and the love we should strive to have for one another. Paul writes,

> **Love** is patient, love is kind. It does not envy, it does not boast, it is not proud. It does not dishonor others, it is not self-seeking, it is not easily angered, it keeps no record of wrongs. Love does not delight in evil but rejoices with the truth. It always protects, always trusts, always hopes, always perseveres.
> Love never fails. **(1 CORINTHIANS 13:4–8)**

Using a pen, circle every characteristic of love you see in the previous passage. These are the qualities we should look for in a close friend or anyone who could have influence over us. Now, we are all works in progress and won't immediately check all these boxes. But the point is, people close to us should draw out and encourage those characteristics in us.

Will this person help you be more patient? Will they encourage you to be kind? Will this person push you to laugh at someone behind their back, or will they inspire you to honor others? These are questions we need to ask as we draw close to people. But guess what? The reverse is true as well—we should be a positive influence on those around us.

Go back and underline the characteristics that you feel like you need to work on.

My dad always says, "Be the person the person you are looking for is looking for." Meaning, the standard we hold for a boyfriend or a friend, we should also hold for ourselves. We should always be working toward being the kind of person who has the characteristics we admire in others. Basically, the ones in the Scripture passage you just read!

But what about the person you decide you won't ever be close to? You realize they aren't the kind of friend you're looking for. Maybe you don't click with them, or maybe they wouldn't be a good influence. Guess what? You are still called to love that person. You don't have to be close. You don't have to go out of your way to invite them over to hang out. But as a Jesus follower, you are still called to love them well.

Let me give you an example. One summer of college, I was working as a camp counselor. I had a cabin full of awesome middle school girls. One girl, however, was a little more of a challenge. She wasn't being kind. She wasn't including everyone. Another girl decided it would only be fair to start treating her the same way. Naturally, this became a big problem, and it turned my entire cabin into a group of bullies.

So I sat everyone down and, without being too specific, gave the challenge that for the rest of the week we were going to love well. We didn't need to become best friends. We didn't need to help plan each other's weddings to each other's brothers. We were just going to love well. So I took out a marker, and on every girl's hand I wrote, "Love well."

Why do I tell you this story? Because no matter who is involved, we are called to *love well*.

## While You Are Close

Okay, here you are—boom—now you are close! Maybe you are dating, or maybe you are close friends. How do you navigate current relationships well?

Again, I have a few questions for you to ask yourself:

- Are you looking to this person to fulfill you?
- Do you make each other better?

### Are You Looking to This Person to Fulfill You?

Believe it or not, we are all on a search for fulfillment and love that can be found only in Christ. But if you're like me, sometimes you're tempted to look to the people around you to fulfill you instead. When I was in high school, I had a best friend who was my world. We did everything together, and she was a really good friend. She pushed me toward Jesus, and we went to church together. On the outside it was a 10/10 friendship. But if she was upset, I was upset. If she was having a good day, I was having a good day. When she would get a new friend, I had a really hard time with that because to me, she was everything. When she couldn't hang out with me, I was at a loss. My mood and my life were dependent on hers, and I looked to her to fulfill me, even though she couldn't (and shouldn't).

It is great to have a best friend, but friends or boyfriends can't be your whole world. It is unfair to put that kind of pressure on a relationship, and ultimately it will cause the relationship to break down.

## Do You Make Each Other Better?

Are you pushing each other toward Jesus or away from Jesus? Are you encouraging each other to make wise choices, or are you doing things that make you want to keep secrets from people you trust? Are you both doing all you can to reflect those characteristics from 1 Corinthians 13 that we talked about earlier? Loving people well is so important. Surrounding yourself with people who love well is important too.

I have two more things for you to think about while you're in close relationships.

### Don't Trade What You Want Most for What You Want in the Moment

There are a lot of things we think we really want. But when we look at those things closely, we may discover that they point to something different.

Let me give you some examples:

> You may think you want attention from that guy, but what you really want is to feel like you are good enough.
> You may think you want to be invited to that party, but what you really want is to feel like you belong.
> You may think you want a boyfriend, but what you really want is to feel valuable.

You see where I'm going with this:

**What** you ultimately want is a life of true authentic love.

Love is being fully known and still chosen. That is the love Jesus offers. That is the love that is patient and kind and delights in the truth.

*Write out some things you think you want:*

_____

_____

_____

*What do those things point to that you ultimately want?*

_____

_____

_____

*How can you get what you ultimately want?*

_____

_____

_____

In John 10:10, Jesus says, "I have come that they may have life, and have it to the full." When you're in a close relationship, don't trade what you want most for what you want in the moment. You get what you ultimately want by drawing near to Jesus and being surrounded by authentic love.

### Don't Let Your Future Be Negatively Influenced by People Who Won't Even Be in Your Future

The truth is, some people are only in our lives temporarily. I know this is hard to believe right now, but as you move through different seasons of your life, your friendships will change. Sure, some of your closest friends will be friends for life. But not all of them!

So if you have a friend or boyfriend who is pushing you away from doing what you know you should do, or toward doing what you know you shouldn't, let them go! Don't let them have a say over your future. They probably won't be in it anyway.

King Solomon, the wisest man ever to live (besides Jesus), wrote proverb after proverb about wisdom and wise people. Listen to this one: "One who walks with wise people will be wise, but a companion of fools will suffer harm" (Proverbs 13:20 NASB). Hang on to the friends who are pushing you to be wise. Hang on to the ones who make you better, who love well and encourage you to do the same. Those are the kinds of friends who *will* be in your future.

## When You Are No Longer Close

The call to love people doesn't break down even if we break up. Let me say that again. The call to love doesn't go away after someone hurts you or leaves you or fades out of your life.

The reality is that most relationships end. Some friends are for a season. In a dating relationship, it either ends or you end up marrying that person someday. If that happens for you, *amazing*! But most people don't marry their middle school, or even high school, sweetheart. So what do we do when a relationship or friendship ends?

You know where I'm going with this: *you still choose to love.*

*Love is kind.* You remain kind to that person and about that person.

*Love does not envy.* You do not become angry or jealous when good things happen to that person.

*Love is not proud.* You do not attempt to "win" the breakup.

*Love does not delight in evil.* You choose not to celebrate their losses.

When I was in high school, I got this all wrong. I was in a

relationship that wasn't pushing me toward love. It ended, and I was sad. I was between hating the guy and wanting to be with the guy. (High school is confusing. You get it.) A mentor told me that I needed to love him from a distance. This meant being kind *about him* but refusing to be *around him*. This was a breakthrough because it showed me that it's possible to exhibit those love characteristics from a distance. That allowed me to protect myself and, at the same time, be kind and considerate in every stage of the relationship.

You want to know what else applies to every season of a relationship? "Let your gentleness be evident to all" (Philippians 4:5). A relationship thrives when gentleness takes the lead. Harsh words, cutting sarcasm, or blatant rudeness is not loving well. Want to love well in every season of a relationship? Let gentleness lead and loving well will be a by-product.

Let's revisit our Scripture passage:

> **Love** is patient, love is kind. It does not envy, it does not boast, it is not proud. It does not dishonor others, it is not self-seeking, it is not easily angered, it keeps no record of wrongs. Love does not delight in evil but rejoices with the truth. It always protects, always trusts, always hopes, always perseveres.
>
> Love never fails. **(1 CORINTHIANS 13:4–8)**

Love never fails.

This truth applies before, during, and after a relationship. Please trust me when I say that following the way of love is how to have deep and meaningful friendships and relationships! And it's also how to experience the love and life that you *ultimately* want.

# CHAPTER 6

# Fear Is *Not* in Charge

I grew up as the youngest in the family, which means I was exposed to some movies that were most likely a little too scary for my age. I did okay with most movies, but one category of scary movies had a strong impact on me. That category? Alien movies.

It started with a *Jimmy Neutron: Boy Genius* episode where aliens abducted all parents from planet Earth and the kids had to rally together to save them. Even as a seven-year-old, I knew I did not have what it takes to save my parents from aliens. (Sorry, Mom and Dad. If that happens, you are on your own.) In time I worked through the whole Jimmy Neutron thing, realizing it makes no sense that aliens would want a bunch of parents on their spaceship. But not too long after that, my alien fears were reignited. I won't name names, but someone in my family—*cough, cough*, the grown man responsible for my emotional and mental development—let me watch a horrifying movie about aliens. To make things worse, after I'd convinced myself I would never go to space, so I didn't need to worry about it, *that same man* took me to see a movie where aliens came to earth. I am not being dramatic when I say I was done for. By the age of eleven, I had developed a real phobia even of the word *alien*. To this day, every time social media tells me there's been another UFO sighting, I have to take deep breaths and listen to soothing music to try to forget.

Maybe you don't have an irrational (or rational) fear of aliens. But in the world we live in, fear is a common feeling. Everyone is afraid of something. We can look down at our phones and be bombarded with things we *should* be afraid of: war, crime, natural disasters—all scary things that can send you spiraling if you give them too much brain space.

And then there are other scary things that may be less severe but are more common. You might find that these fears hit a little closer to home:

- the fear of being left out
- the fear of being abandoned
- the fear of failing
- the fear of being embarrassed
- the fear of missing out
- the fear of what other people will think of you
- the fear of losing people you love

Go ahead and break out a pen and circle any of these you have felt in the past few weeks. Feel free to add a few of your own in the margins.

If you're like me, you probably circled more than one. Fear is rampant, and it feels like if we think too hard about anything, we can spiral into a puddle of anxiety over the what-ifs.

I want to take a moment here to address something important. Anxiety and depression are unfortunately a reality for many of us. Clinical anxiety is *not* what we are about to talk about in this chapter. As someone who has struggled with a panic disorder and has had seasons of deep anxiety, I know firsthand the frustration that comes from people slapping a "just trust God" sticker on me and moving on.

If you struggle with clinical anxiety, I want to encourage you to do three things:

1. Talk to a parent, a mentor, or someone you trust.
2. Get into counseling.
3. Use what I'm about to talk about as a supplement to more structured help.

Struggling with mental health can feel isolating and scary. I want you to know you are not alone and there is so much hope for getting better.

An interesting thing about fear is that it doesn't always stay on the inside. It isn't always hidden. Fear can be physical. In most cases, fear *is* physical. The reaction to fear is a biological reaction. God put it into our bodies so that if a bear is ever chasing us, we run. We naturally take quick action! When you are afraid, your body reacts. Your heart rate may increase. You may feel blood rush to your face or even feel fluttering in your stomach. Since fear is not all in your head, but also in your body, it can push you to make decisions or act in a certain way.

Let me give you some examples. I am slightly afraid of birds. It's not a fear of birds in the sky but of birds that seem to have no fear of me. I think this stems from the time my grandfather told me that if I ever encounter a small animal that doesn't seem afraid of me, it probably has rabies. I doubt he was lumping birds into that category, but regardless, if a bird comes too close, my heart rate increases and I want to get away from that bird. That fear causes some physical reactions. I back away. I hide behind someone. Or I give in and give the bird the french fry I know he's asking for. For the record, I don't recommend that approach. It makes the problem worse. Then the bird's friends come too. That's terrifying.

See there? My fear creates an action in me. This is also the case for less physical fears. For example, the first day of my freshman year of high school, I walked through the doors of my new school confident and excited about having a great year. That was until about two minutes in, when my friend ran up to me, tripped, and fell on top of me, and then we both proceeded to topple over in the middle of the hallway. Strong start to my high school career. I was so embarrassed and was certain that everyone had seen the fiasco. My reaction to being thoroughly embarrassed was an immediate swirling fear that it could happen again. All of that caused me to say some not-so-kind things to that friend.

Whether it's a physical fear or more of an emotional fear, *fear pushes us to act*. And most of the time, our reaction to fear doesn't lead us where we want to go. It causes us to run or flail our arms around like a crazy person (the bird thing) or to lash out at a friend whose only offense was being a bit uncoordinated.

Fears can cause us to act:

- When we are afraid of being left out, we may leave others out to secure our spot.
- When we are afraid of being abandoned, we may compromise our values to get someone we care about to stay.
- When we are afraid of failing, we may cheat.
- When we are afraid of losing our reputation, we may change who we are in order for people to like us.

Even though fear pushes us to act, the key is to refrain from acting in a way that is destructive to us or the people around us. In

Tindell Baldwin's book, *Popular*, she tells the heartbreaking story of her journey through her high school years as she was filled with hidden fears. Fears of missing out on what seemed most important at the time—being popular, being accepted, gaining attention, and being included. Fears of not being *the best* and not measuring up to her brothers, who seemed perfect. Those fears drove her to make decisions that wreaked havoc in her life and took time to heal and recover from.

Tindell is a friend of ours. She's a beautiful wife and mom, and she leverages her story any chance she gets as she disciples high school girls and encourages them not to let their fears be the boss of them. Honestly, *fear is bossy*. Fear takes who we are, and who God wants us to be, and turns us into someone we may not even recognize.

So what do we do? Well, throughout Scripture, we see the words "do not fear" over and over again. Simple enough? Just stop being afraid. Cool, got it. Okay, chapter over. Thanks, bye.

Obviously, I'm kidding. It isn't that simple. But there are some simple truths that can help:

- God loves us.
- God provides for us.
- God has good plans for us.

These truths are important, and I want you to hold on to them! Let's break these down.

## We Can Trust That God Loves Us

Here's a mind-blowing truth about God: *While we are unable to love perfectly, he is able.* And once again, through Paul's pen, God tells us what real love looks like:

> **Love** is patient, love is kind. It does not envy, it does not boast, it is not proud. It does not dishonor others, it is not self-seeking, it is not easily angered, it keeps no record of wrongs. Love does not delight in evil but rejoices with the truth. It always protects, always trusts, always hopes, always perseveres.
>
> Love never fails. **(1 CORINTHIANS 13:4–8)**

That's the kind of love our heavenly Father has for us. A love that demonstrates patience. A love that models kindness. A love that isn't centered on self. A love that isn't distracted by pride and arrogance. A love that honors. A love that is generous. A love that doesn't get angry and lash out. A love that chooses not to hold on to our misdeeds. A love that protects us and fights for us. A love that believes in us. And a love that stays *near*.

## We Can Trust That God Provides for Us

God's provision doesn't usually come packaged the way we expect, or even the way we might prefer. Often it's not until long after a situation resolves that we are able to see that *his* way and *his* timing were much better than what we had hoped.

Check out this verse that comes a little later in our Philippians 4 passage: "My God will meet all your needs according to the riches of his glory in Christ Jesus" (v. 19). The people Paul was writing to were worried that if they were generous to others, they might not have enough for themselves. In this verse, Paul is reminding them that they don't need to worry. He had experienced firsthand how God provides. He tells them that God knows what they need and will meet those needs. He can be trusted to provide.

## We Can Trust That God Has Good Plans for Us

**We** are God's handiwork, created in Christ Jesus to do good works, which God prepared in advance for us to do. **(EPHESIANS 2:10)**

Did you know you are God's handiwork? Another way to say it is that you are his "workmanship." He created you with purpose. He created you *with* purpose and *for* a purpose. It's amazing that the God who created the world and everything in it created you intentionally, with a purpose and a plan just for you!

I want to give you one more tool for when fear strikes. In Philippians 4:5, Paul makes this small but mighty statement: "The Lord is near."

That's a short sentence, but it packs so much meaning. Let's take a closer look.

First, let's remind ourselves who the Lord is. He is:

- all-powerful
- all-knowing
- fully good

What does it mean that God is near? Paul is saying that the God who can do anything, who knows everything, and who is completely good is *with you* and has a plan *for you*. When we believe that truth, everything we are afraid of becomes smaller, right?

You see, *nearness creates peace*. You know this. When a child is afraid, they cry out and a parent or a caretaker comes. Just the nearness of a safe person calms a fearful child.

As Jesus followers, we have access to God's nearness twenty-four hours a day, seven days a week, every single week! God is with you. More than that, God has a plan for your life.

Let's be real for a second though. Even people who follow Jesus have tough times. That's the nature of the world we live in. But let's be reminded of what we know. In the past chapters, we talked about how Jesus went to the cross for us. Remember what that means? It means that Jesus defeated death. So even in the hardest situations, death is *not* the end.

If we follow the trajectory of our fears and let them play out to a worst-case scenario, some of them lead to death. Physical death maybe. But also social death, emotional death, mental death, and death of relationships. So realizing that Jesus defeated death should shrink our fears so they become much smaller than what we thought they were. If a loved one passes away, because of what Jesus did, we can be confident that this is not the end, that we will see them again someday. If something happens and we lose all our friends, we can have hope that God has a plan for us and we will make new friends. If we fail at something or do something embarrassing, we can know God loves us unconditionally and will never abandon us.

When we look at our fears through the lens of God's nearness, they're not so overwhelming. So what does that look like practically?

1. Remember that God is near. Start with memorizing this short verse: "The Lord is near." When you come face-to-face with fear and your body starts reacting, take some deep breaths and say out loud, or under your breath, "The Lord is near. The Lord is near. The Lord is near."

2. Don't let fear boss you around. Notice when you feel afraid, and don't let your fear tell you what to do. Get in the habit

of asking yourself this question: "Am I making this decision based on fear?" Another way to say this is "Am I saying this out of fear?" or "Am I doing this out of fear?" Take a moment, examine your actions, and see if you are letting fear boss you around.

3. Reflect on your fears. Why are you afraid of what you are afraid of? How does God meet that need for you? As humans, we have the ability to think about what we are thinking about. Confusing? Let me say it another way. You and I are able to get to the bottom of our own thoughts. That means we can notice when we are feeling afraid and really ask ourselves why. Why does this person make me nervous? Why does this situation cause dread? And then we can take what we have learned, cast our fears onto God, and let him help us through them.

Fear is real. Fear is understandable. But we don't have to be slaves to fear. Jesus has already conquered death on our behalf, so we don't have to be afraid. *The Lord is near.*

CHAPTER 7

# Peace in the Chaos

Sometimes I am my own worst enemy. Let me tell you what I mean. I have the heart of a chill, laid-back, everything-is-going-to-work-out-fine person, but I have the brain of a high-achieving perfectionist who thinks being late should be a federal crime.

In high school this combination made for very stressful mornings. Here's how they would go. I would hit snooze eight times because my heart would tell me that I deserved to sleep and I could totally get ready for school in four minutes and twenty-five seconds. When I would finally get out of bed, my brain would kick in and panic. *Okay, you no longer have time to shower, and you slept in a ponytail so your hair is all creased and weird* (because my heart told me the night before that everything would be fine and I would have plenty of time to shower). So my brain would boss me around for fifteen minutes until I was presentable-*ish*, and then I would *run* (not walk) downstairs to a pleasant mother who had made a nice breakfast and had no idea that her creased-haired daughter was about to wreak havoc on her peaceful morning. Alas, I would declare that there was no time for breakfast and also, "Mom, how could you not wake me up!" Of course, my brain blamed my mother for everything because, duh, she and her four-course breakfast were obviously the villain of the situation.

I would then get in the car only to come face-to-face with my brain's worst-case scenario—traffic. Then the stress would set in. I would be sitting in that car stressed that my first-period teacher would hate me because I was going to be one minute late for class. I was also stressed that I wouldn't have time to run to my locker to grab my books for second period, and then I'd remember my locker was so far away from my second-period class that there was no way I would be able to get the books after first period and make it there on time. So then I was stressed that my second-period teacher would hate me too. Then during lunch my first- and second-period teachers would probably hang out and plot a way to make sure I couldn't get into college.

So now I was stressed thinking I would have to work at Chick-fil-A my whole life (honestly, there are worse places to work). *But, oh shoot! I don't know how to make waffle fries.* Then I'd google how to make waffle fries because I was stressed I was going to be bad at the only job I would ever be able to have because of . . . traffic.

Yeah, I am a delight in the mornings.

My hope is that your mornings aren't typically as chaotic as mine were, but if they are, no shame. We do our best. Regardless of your morning routine, there is one thing I know to be true for all of us: *stress is real.*

I want to take a second to validate your stress. Adults may look at you and tell you, "These are the easiest years of your life." Hearing that is unhelpful and discouraging because I know many of you are stressed to the max. What society puts on you as a young girl is rough. You're expected to have good grades, be a good friend, be involved in clubs, play a sport after school, do all your homework, have a good relationship with your family, go to church, spend time with God, read your Bible, read other books, have a hobby, have a creative outlet, eat healthy meals, look pretty, do your makeup, do your hair, be cute, be up to date on the TV show everyone is watching, plan your future. . . oh, and also have fun! Enjoy your life while you are young!

Honestly, it's all too much.

Take a second to list a few things you find yourself stressing about:

_____

_____

_____

You have a lot on your plate. Whether it's work or relationships or pressure from your family, it's not healthy to live in a constant state of stress. Plenty of studies show that chronic stress wreaks havoc on your body and mind if it's not taken care of. So what do we do? Over the next few pages, we'll talk about three ways to help ease the pressure and get a handle on all that stress.

## Guard Your Time

Society puts unrealistic expectations on you. Read that again. Society puts unrealistic expectations on you. You can't live your life with the goal of living up to the expectations that our culture places on teenage girls. Trying to do that will cause you to live a life bogged down by stress and pressure. So what do you do?

You stop.

You say no.

You guard your time.

There are four categories you can put your responsibilities into: nonnegotiables, priorities, possibilities, and NO.

Let me show you an example:

### Nonnegotiables (Things You Literally Have to Do)

go to school

eat

sleep

### Priorities (Things You Should Do)

do homework

hang out with your family

hang out with your friends

pursue your personal relationship with Jesus

go to church

### Possibilities (Things You Want to Do)

sports

hobbies

### NO

anything you currently do that you should start saying no to

In the "Meet Me in the Middle" section, you are going to get practical and categorize your responsibilities with your mom. Creating margin in your schedule will drastically reduce your stress because you will no longer be running from thing to thing and you can instead stop to enjoy the things you are saying yes to.

## Guard Your Hope

We are going to do a fun little activity. We are going to follow our stress all the way to the end result. I'm serious. We are going to look our stress right in the face and get to the bottom of it. The goal is to answer the question, What would happen if what we are most stressed about came true? But don't worry, I'll go first.

**What are you most stressed about?**
Losing my friends.

**Why are you stressed about that?**
I love my friends.
Being rejected is hurtful.
I don't want to be alone.

**What is the worst thing that could happen?**
My friends could hate me and tell everything I have ever told them to everyone in school and then everyone would turn against me and I'd have to be pulled out of school because I'm being bullied so much.

**Then what?**
I would have to go to a new school and start over.

Okay, we made it to the end. Having to go to a new school because I've been bullied is bad, but honestly, I could probably handle that. I'd still have my family. God would still love me. I think I'd be okay.

Getting to the end of the stress injects hope into the stress.

And hope leads to peace.

More on that in a second. It's your turn!

**What are you most stressed about?**

_____

_____

_____

**Why are you stressed about that?**

_____

_____

_____

*What is the* worst *thing that could happen?*

_____

_____

_____

*Then what?*

_____

_____

_____

I wish I could sit with each one of you and point to the individual hope that your stress lands on, but there is one hope that all Jesus followers have:

God loves you.
God is with you.
Jesus defeated death.

A lot of your stressors may end with:

- being hated
- being alone
- death

The truth is that Jesus 100 percent conquered every one of our worst-case scenarios. Because of that, you can have hope. Our hope and our peace rest securely on the foundation of Jesus Christ. His promises are certain and are not going away. Nothing is more powerful. Nothing is surer. Here are Jesus's own words. In this passage, he had just explained to his disciples that some hard times were coming: "These things I have spoken to you so that in Me you may have peace. In the world you have tribulation, but take courage; I have overcome the world" (John 16:33 NASB).

**The** bigger our hope is, the smaller our stressors are.

We have the ultimate hope. When we put what stresses us out next to the hope we have in Jesus, nothing compares.

## Guard Your Heart

Our last point in dealing with stress brings us back to our Philippians passage. Look at what Paul writes:

**Do** not be anxious about anything, but in every situation, by prayer and petition, with thanksgiving, present your requests to God. And the peace of God, which transcends all understanding, will guard your hearts and your minds in Christ Jesus. **(PHILIPPIANS 4:6–7)**

There's a lot to unpack in these two verses. And it's connected to a promise. Let's break it down.

"Do not be anxious about anything" (v. 6). Sound easy? Sure! Just don't worry. Don't be stressed. Ha! Yeah right.

- The big test coming up? Not a problem. It's only 50 percent of your grade. No worries.
- Tryouts for the varsity soccer team? Eh, you'll be fine!
- A family member going into major surgery? Just don't think about it.

Obviously, those responses are nowhere near realistic. And

they are far from the goal. Paul's instruction not to be anxious isn't about pretending nothing stressful is going on. Rather, step by step he tells us exactly what to do: "But in every situation, by prayer and petition, with thanksgiving, present your requests to God" (v. 6).

Here is where the work begins. Find a quiet spot. Grab a pen and notebook. Or simply do this the moment a big stressor is staring you in the face!

Step one: Thank God.

Huh? I thought we were talking about stress. Allie, you want me to thank God for my stress? Not exactly. Take a moment to refocus—taking your eyes *off* the stressor and putting them *on* what you do have. Can't think of anything to thank God for? Here are some ideas:

- Thank him for allowing you to come to him at any moment.
- Thank him for any blessings associated with the stress.
- Thank him for what he's going to do, whether it's soon or whether it's later.
- Thank him for his promise that he is *with you* in it.
- Thank him for the hope you have in Jesus.

Step two: Present your request.

What is it you want? Do you want peace? Do you want an A? Do you want your friends to forgive you? Do you want confidence? Take a moment to figure out exactly what the stress is, and turn it into a request. How often do we stress about it, talk about it, worry about it, cry about it and never actually ask God to help us with it? That's why we put a stake in the ground and ask God to move.

What do you get in return? "And the peace of God, which transcends all understanding, will guard your hearts and your minds in Christ Jesus" (v. 7). Paul tells us that God will grant us peace. Peace that doesn't make sense. Peace that doesn't always match our circumstances.

Stress is something we deal with every day. We tend to let one outside factor get into our brain and wiggle around in there until we are unhinged and overwhelmed. That is why having this tool in your back pocket is crucial. I go through this passage and this formula at least once a day.

Take this morning for instance. I've had a crazy week and have not had time to do all the things I need to do. When I look at my to-do list, my natural reaction is to freak out. My body wants to go into go-go-go mode and do everything as fast as possible and ignore the people around me. So what do I do? I do exactly what Paul telling us to do in the following passage:

**Do** not be anxious about anything, but in every situation, by prayer and petition, with thanksgiving, present your requests to God. And the peace of God, which transcends all understanding, will guard your hearts and your minds in Christ Jesus. **(PHILIPPIANS 4:6–7)**

Here is a personal example from my journal:

**With thanksgiving:** God, thank you for my job. Thank you for my family. Thank you that I have a house and a garbage disposal.

**Present your requests to God:** Lord, give me what I need to do the things you have for me to do. Help me to carve out time to get some things done while also finding joy in my day.

**And the peace of God, which transcends all understanding, will guard your hearts and your minds in Christ Jesus:** Now I will walk in your peace and listen to you and not allow my heart to be stressed.

Now it's your turn:

**With thanksgiving:**

_____

_____

_____

**Present your requests to God:**

_____

_____

_____

**And the peace of God, which transcends all understanding, will guard your hearts and your minds in Christ Jesus:**

_____

_____

_____

I promise God will meet you in your prayer and grant you peace that doesn't make sense in your stressful moments.

God is bigger than any problems that come our way. He is sovereign and in control of everything. And he offers us peace. In the midst of the storms, he offers peace. In the face of danger, he offers peace. Even in the busyness and chaos of life, he offers peace. And get this. His peace *takes action* in this verse. God's peace, which doesn't make sense to the world, *does* something. It's active. It guards our hearts, and it guards our minds.

So to protect our hearts, we thank God, make a request, and let God's peace guard us.

I know stress is prevalent in our lives. So to close this chapter, I want to offer a small prayer you can pray when you feel especially stressed: "Father, your ways are better and higher. Thank you for your hope and peace. *Help me do what I can do and to release the rest to you.*"

# CHAPTER 8

# Writing a Good Story

Hi, hello, wow! You've made it to the final chapter. First of all, I am proud of you. I can't tell you how many books I have started and not finished. So if you are here, you should be proud of yourself.

So far we have covered quite a range of topics. We have talked about your personal relationship with God, your identity, comparison, family, friends, boys, fears, and stress! In this chapter we are going to take Paul's final instruction in our Philippians 4 passage and "put it into practice" (v. 9). We are going to make a plan. We are going to take all the topics, all the conversations you've had with your mom over the past few weeks, and put them into practice.

How do we do this? We put them into practice through our decision-making. We make thousands of decisions every single day. I know it sounds like I'm exaggerating, but I'm not. Studies have been done about it.

Here are some examples of the everyday decisions you might make:

- Should I hit snooze? Should I hit snooze *again*?
- What am I going to wear? This one leads to about thirty more decisions by the time you're dressed.

- What will I have for breakfast? Again, multiple decisions are made by the time food is in your stomach.
- When will I do my homework?
- Will I talk to this person?
- When I pass that borderline stranger in the hallway, will I look straight ahead or smile?
- Will I laugh at that joke I don't really think is funny?
- Will I join in the circle of gossip even though I know I shouldn't?
- Will I text that person back?
- How will I spend my time after I get home?

The list goes on and on.

Take a second to jot down some decisions you have already had to make today.

_____

_____

_____

Sometimes our decisions are simple right-versus-wrong kinds of decisions. Like, should I cheat on this test? It seems like everyone else is cheating! Or should I share the secret that my friend made me promise not to tell? In these cases, there *is* a right answer and a wrong one. These decisions should be fairly easy to make. But some decisions are harder to sort through. Maybe because we have a preference but also an inkling that our preference is the wrong decision. Or because other people are encouraging us in a certain direction, but we're not sure their motives are right. Or because occasionally there's more than one good choice and we just don't know which way to go. These decisions are harder to make.

We also know that some decisions carry more weight than others. The clothes you decide to wear on Monday probably won't have the same importance as who you decide to hang out with over the weekend. Whether you choose a smoothie or go for scrambled eggs and bacon for breakfast doesn't ultimately matter as much as the words and tone you use when talking to your friend.

So as those who want to grow their faith in Jesus and follow the way of Philippians 4:4–9, what do we do? How do we become good decision-makers? How do we get in the habit of making the kinds of decisions that show we're serious about following Jesus? We start with being aware of how important our decisions are. They matter. They matter now, but they also matter for our future.

What if I told you that the decisions you make today could affect where you end up twenty years from now? *Whoa, whoa, whoa, that seems kind of dramatic, Allie.* You're not wrong—it *is* dramatic. But also true.

So take a moment to think about your future. Dream. Process. Go there for a second and jot down a few answers.

In twenty years:

*What do you want your life to look like (job, location, hobbies, goals, etc.)?*

_____

_____

_____

*What people do you want to have in your life?*

_____

_____

_____

*What words do you want people to use when they describe you?*

_____

_____

_____

*What do you want to have accomplished?*

_____

_____

_____

*Who do you want to be?*

_____

_____

_____

My mom presents a similar version of this exercise to your mom, using the question, *What story do you want to tell?* I decided to split that question into bite-size pieces by using the previous questions.

But really, the decisions we make now *do* write the stories of our lives. I bet I can guess something about you: you hope your life is a collection of stories you want to tell. Nobody wants chapters of their lives to be stories they feel like they have to hide or be embarrassed about later. I'm not saying that choosing to have a PB&J for lunch is going to affect where you end up in twenty years, but it is important to know that you don't magically end up somewhere one day.

My dad says all the time, "Direction determines destination." In other words, the steps you take and the direction in which you are going determine where you end up. It's a principle—something that's true whether or not we realize it. It just *is.*

So in what direction are you going? Are you headed toward the destination you want? Are you going toward God? Are you moving closer to the people you want to have in your life in twenty years? Are you making decisions that align with what you want to be known for? These are important questions that you get to decide how to answer right now.

It's true that there are a lot of decisions you don't get to make right now. Some things are simply outside your control. You may not get to choose your school or what's for dinner or even where you are allowed to go in this season of your life. But you *do* get to choose the direction your life is going in, and that's a pretty big deal! So pick your destination and start making decisions that keep you moving in that direction.

Okay, there's a second question that's important to ask as you try to make great decisions. This second question is also a big one. Super important. It works like a filter and can help you write the story you want to tell and be the person you want to be. That question is, *What is the wise thing to do?*

Before we jump right into wisdom, let's pause a second and talk about regret. Regret is like a weight. After we make a poor decision, regret is the emotion related to the consequences of that poor choice. It hangs around our neck like a literal weight sometimes. When we find ourselves faced with regret, it's often pretty easy to see where we went wrong. If we pause and look back, we usually realize that our regret was preceded by a *series* of unwise decisions. Take a look at this example:

> "There's nothing *wrong* with hanging out with her, even though she's known for making bad decisions. Maybe she needs a friend."
> ➔ "There's nothing really *wrong* with punting our studying and shooting a TikTok video with her instead!"
> ➔ "It's not going to kill anyone if I peek at the test she got from the teacher's desk, since we didn't get around to studying yesterday."
> ➔ "Now I feel guilty about cheating. I've never done that before. I wish I hadn't."

You can see how the gap incrementally closes and how we baby-step right up to the line between *not exactly wrong* and *absolutely wrong.* If we had stopped at the very first decision and asked, "What is the *wise* thing to do?" and answered it honestly, we wouldn't have started hanging out with someone who would negatively influence us. And we wouldn't be holding the weight of regret that came with cheating.

The beauty of the wisdom question is that it backs us away from that sometimes-magnetic line: *How close can I get to doing wrong without actually doing wrong?* The wisdom question says, "Hey! Hey! Step back from the line! Your toes are dangling over the edge, and it won't take much to push you over to the place where regret lives."

You can see how important wisdom is in our decision-making.

The *Lexham Bible Dictionary* says that being wise "refers to practical skills associated with understanding and living a successful life."[13] See that? Even the Bible dictionary wants you to live a successful life. And to get there, wisdom is required. How do we get wisdom, you ask? James lays out the answer clearly: "If any of you lacks wisdom, you should ask God, who gives generously to all without finding fault, and it will be given to you" (James 1:5).

You want wisdom? Ask God for it, James says. Simple as that.

When you're faced with a decision, ask yourself, "What is the wise thing to do?" If you don't have an immediate answer, that's okay. Ask God! He may give you clarity through Scripture during your quiet time. Or he'll speak to you though your parents, or a wise counselor, or a friend in your path. Or he'll simply bring clarity out of the chaos of your thoughts. He'll whisper wisdom to you when you have yourself in a position to hear. And often, in simply asking for wisdom, you're positioned to hear.

Here's another amazing truth about wisdom. It is one of the attributes of God that is available to us through the Holy Spirit, who lives in us. And he delights in illuminating our way, even in our mundane day-to-day decision-making.

Because I care about you, I want to let you know something important. The wise thing to do is not always the easy thing to do. It is not always the popular thing to do. It might upset some people. You see, as Jesus followers, we are called to look different. We are called to act different. We are called to make different decisions than the people around us. And that can be difficult.

When I was in high school, I experienced this firsthand. Because I was a theater kid in public high school, I found myself in a friend group with a lot of people who were really different than I was. People who did not follow Jesus and people who seemed a lot cooler than me. Because I was friends with them, I would be invited to do fun things and go to cool places, most of which were fun and harmless. But around my senior year, the places they wanted to go and things they wanted to do became a lot *less* harmless. And I had a decision to make. I could go and do my best not to partake. Or I could look at what I wanted my future to be and ask, "What is the wise thing to do?"

Let's just say, I started saying no a lot more. I would make other plans so I would be "busy then." Or if I was feeling brave, I would simply say, "You know, I don't think I want to be a part of that." Honestly, that led to some lonely Friday nights. But where I am now is exactly where I want to be! Looking back, I am so happy with the decisions I made. And I promise you will be too.

Here is a simple prayer you can borrow from me: "Lord, give me the wisdom to *know* what's right and the courage to *do* what's right even when it's hard. And even if I have to do it by myself."

You won't regret that prayer!

# Final Thoughts
# for Daughters

Well, friends, you did it! Thank you so much for leaning in and embarking on this journey with your mom and also with me.

My hope and prayer is that through these pages and the interactions you had with your mom, you were able to grow your personal faith and it has started to spill over into every aspect of your life.

As a backdrop to all the topics, we focused on this passage from Philippians 4:4–9:

> **Rejoice** in the Lord always. I will say it again: Rejoice! Let your gentleness be evident to all. The Lord is near. Do not be anxious about anything, but in every situation, by prayer and petition, with thanksgiving, present your requests to God. And the peace of God, which transcends all understanding, will guard your hearts and your minds in Christ Jesus. Finally, brothers and sisters, whatever is true, whatever is noble, whatever is right, whatever is pure, whatever is lovely, whatever is admirable—if anything is excellent or praiseworthy—think about such

things. Whatever you have learned or received or heard from me, or seen in me—put it into practice. And the God of peace will be with you.

It can be hard to absorb everything we talked about over the past eight chapters, so I want to do a bite-size recap of every chapter to remind you of how you can bring your faith into each of these areas of your life.

For the last time, break out a pen and circle in the list below the pieces of advice that you feel have positively affected your life so far, and underline the ones you feel you still need to work on.

Here we go:

**Chapter 1:** Spend time with God every day, and learn, apply, and continue in the truth of God's Word.

**Chapter 2:** To help you remember that you are who God says you are, keep truth in front of you and live out your identity.

**Chapter 3:** To beat the comparison game, celebrate what God has given others and leverage what God has given you.

**Chapter 4:** When it comes to your family, you can choose to appreciate, choose to forgive, and choose gentleness.

**Chapter 5:** Find your people by choosing to love in every season.

**Chapter 6:** Remember that fear doesn't get to make decisions for you because you have the God of the universe on your side, and he loves you, provides for you, and has good plans for you.

**Chapter 7:** Fight stress by guarding your time, guarding your hope, and guarding your heart.

**Chapter 8:** To get where you want to go in life, ask yourself, "What story do I want to tell?" and "What is the wise thing to do?" and head in that direction.

Thank you for going on this beautiful, wonderful journey with my mom and me. Deepening your faith is the most important investment you can make . As always, remember that you are not alone. You have people who love you; your heavenly Father, who is with you; and your mom, who thinks you're really awesome!

,

## Allie

# Acknowledgments

## From Sandra and Allie

Thank you to the team at HarperCollins for your confidence in us, your insights, and your ideas to make this book *so much* better. Thank you, Keren Baltzer, for your trusty editing and diligent corrections. You've been amazing.

Thank you to Suzy Gray. Nothing that gets done would get done without you. Not only are you the smartest person we know, but your smile and your laugh make everything brighter, better, and more fun.

Thank you to all the moms—and the grandmothers, aunts, and mentors—for taking time to invest in a young lady important to you. Your thumbprint on her life will bear fruit beyond what you may see in the short term.

And thank you to our heavenly Father. May we always be daughters who bring you joy.

## From Sandra

Thank you to my amazing husband, Andy, for your encouragement, love, and listening ear as I bounced ideas your way for trusted insight. Gosh, I love you.

And to my precious Allie. You are the daughter every mom

dreams of. How blessed I am that you're mine, and how fun to do a first project together!

## From Allie

Thank you to each girl who dove in and decided to entrust us with your time and attention. Thank you to my sweet husband, Clay, who listened and laughed and supported me through this entire process. Thank you to my mom, whom I admire and look up to more than you will ever know. I loved every moment of doing this project with you!

# Notes

1. Robert S. McGee, *The Search for Significance: Seeing Your True Worth through God's Eyes* (Nashville: W Publishing Group, 2003), 27.
2. Nancy Leigh DeMoss, *A Place of Quiet Rest: Finding Intimacy with God Through a Daily Devotional Life* (Chicago: Moody, 2000), 44.
3. Andy Stanley, *The New Rules for Love, Sex, and Dating* (Grand Rapids: Zondervan, 2014), 51.
4. Stanley, *New Rules for Love*, 48.
5. Chuck Swindoll, *Simple Faith* (Nashville: W Publishing Group, 2003), 47.
6. "Glossophobia Be Gone: 5 Methods to Curb Speech Anxiety," King University Online, May 27, 2020, https://online.king.edu /news/glossophobia-gone/.
7. John Burke, *Imagine Heaven: Near-Death Experiences, God's Promises, and the Exhilarating Future That Awaits You* (Grand Rapids: Baker, 2015), 77.
8. L. B. Cowman, *Streams in the Desert: 366 Daily Devotional Readings*, ed. Jim Reimann (Grand Rapids: Zondervan, 2016), 268.
9. "Any Anxiety Disorder," National Institute of Mental Health, accessed October 30, 2023, https://www.nimh.nih.gov/health /statistics/any-anxiety-disorder#part_155096.
10. Dr. Joel Hoomans, "35,000 Decisions: The Great Choices of Strategic Leaders," Roberts Wesleyan University, March 20, 2015, https:// go.roberts.edu/leadingedge/the-great-choices-of-strategic-leaders.

11. Andy Stanley, *Better Decisions, Fewer Regrets: 5 Questions to Help You Determine Your Next Move* (Grand Rapids: Zondervan, 2020), 60.

12. *The Oxford Pocket Dictionary of Current English*, s.v. "second nature," Encyclopedia.com, accessed September 20, 2023, https://www.encyclopedia.com/humanities/dictionaries-thesauruses-pictures-and-press-releases/second-nature.

13. Martin A. Shields, "Wisdom," *Lexham Bible Dictionary*, ed. John D. Barry et al. (Bellingham, WA: Lexham, 2016).

# Parenting

## Getting It Right

*Andy and Sandra Stanley*

Am I getting parenting right? Most parents, at any and every stage, find themselves asking this question.

Whether you're sleep deprived with a colicky newborn or navigating the emotional roller coaster of a teenager, parenting has its ups and downs, its confusion and clarity, its big blowups, and small victories. And no matter our family makeup or our children's personalities, many of us experience anxiety over our children's futures and often fear making a mistake.

In *Parenting: Getting It Right*, Andy and Sandra combine their experience and wisdom into a guide that helps readers understand and live by essential parenting principles. In an inviting, conversational approach that is both informative and accessible, the Stanleys help readers understand the most important goal in parenting and learn the steps to pursue it by:

- Learning the four distinct stages of parenting
- Clarifying the primary goal of parenting and developing a parenting orientation around that goal
- Identifying and adapting their approach—not their rules—to their children's distinct personalities
- Deciding on their short list of nonnegotiables and learning to stick to it

You don't have to constantly doubt if you're getting it right as a parent. Start here and feel confident about raising a healthy and happy family.

*Available in stores and online!*